Hydroponic Gardening

DIY Beginners Guide for Build Your Healthy Own Fruits, Herbs, and Vegetables Growing System

Peter Bradley

Table of Contents

INTRODUCTION

Hydroponic gardening can be VERY complex, with sensors and computers controlling everything from watering cycles to nutrient power and the total amount of light the plants get. On the flip side, hydroponics may also be incredibly straightforward, such as a hand watered bucket of sand growing one plant can also be a way of hydroponic gardening.

Many hobby-oriented hydroponics systems are somewhere between the two extremes mentioned previously. The "average" home hydroponic system generally contains a couple of basic components: a growing tray, a reservoir, an easy timer controlled submersible pump to water the plants and an air pump and air stone to oxygenate the nutrient solution. Obviously, light (either artificial or natural) is also required.

Now, much of the food on the dinner table is homegrown. There's a certain satisfaction in knowing the food on your plate is increased by using your skills. You don't need a massive budget to start, and once you start, you'll quickly taste and feel the advantages. As a result of the success of hydroponics, you've now got plenty of herbs, salad, fruits and other ingredients.

It might be you're just beginning. You might even have a little flat, as I formerly had. In both cases, if you'd like a quick climbing, bountiful harvest, subsequently hydroponics is the thing to do. Have a peek at the first advantages if you grow your own food with hydroponics: You do not need a lawn or garden area.

Plants grow faster and create more harvest when compared with plants grown in soil. You can grow out of season plants, all year round. You can grow special plants in almost any climate. If that is not enough to seal the bargain, how about not getting soil under your fingernails?

This eBook, therefore, will assist individuals who are in an identical situation and offer advice about the best way to select the very best hydroponic system and crop for homegrown food yearlong. Indoors, in a greenhouse, or outside, there's a hydroponic method of growing for all kinds of gardeners.

History and Definition of Hydroponics

Hydroponics simply means working water ("hydro" means "water" and "ponos" signifies "labor"). Many distinct civilizations have used hydroponic growing techniques: hanging gardens of Babylon, the floating gardens of the Aztecs of Mexico and people of the Chinese are cases of the 'Hydroponic' culture.

Hydroponics is of course a new way of growing plants. But giant strides have been created through the past few years in this innovative field of agriculture. Through the past century, both scientists and horticulturists have experimented with various techniques of hydroponics. Among the possible uses of hydroponics that drove research was for growing fresh produce in nonarable regions of the Earth.

It's a simple actuality that some individuals can't grow in the soil within their place (if there's any soil in it at all). This application of hydroponics was analyzed during World War II. Troops stationed on nonarable islands in the Pacific were provided with fresh produce grown in locally based hydroponic systems.

Later in the century, hydroponics was integrated to the space program. As NASA believed the practicalities of finding a society on a different plant or the planet's moon, hydroponics readily fit into their sustainability aims. This study is continuing. However, by the 1970s, it was not only analysts and scientists who had been included in hydroponics. Traditional farmers and keen hobbyists started to be drawn to the virtues of hydroponic growing. Some of the positive aspects of hydroponics comprise:

- The ability to create higher yields than traditional, soil-based agriculture
- Letting food be grown and eaten in regions of the world that may not support plants in the soil
- Eliminating the requirement for massive pesticide usage (considering most insects reside in the soil), effectively making our soil, air, food, and water cleaner
-

Commercial growers are now flocking to hydroponics like never before. The ideals enclosing these climbing techniques touch on subjects that most men and women care about, like helping end world hunger and also making the world cleaner.

Besides the extensive research that's happening, everyday folks from all around the world are constructing (or buying) their particular systems to grow great-tasting, fresh food to their loved ones members and friends. Educators are realizing that the remarkable software that hydroponics could have in the classroom. And ambitious people are trying to make their fantasies come true by growing their living in their own garden oceans, selling their produce to local restaurants and markets.

Can Plants Grow Without Soil? Hydroponic Gardening is the Solution!

Hydroponic Gardening is the method where crops can grow without soil. Using hydroponics to grow plants can be good for many growers, as it enables plants to be grown much faster and most times with less difficulties.

Plants are grown in a solution made up of water and dissolved nutrients necessary for the specific plant. There are lots of hydroponics systems and techniques which are utilized in growing plants that are now booming.

The different kinds of hydroponics systems and techniques include the nutrient film technique (or NFT), aeroponics, and the aeration technique.

With the aeroponics techniques, plants are fastened utilizing rigid pipes, films, or screens. The nutrients are circulated to the plants' water source and the plants' roots are suspended inside the water. The plant subsequently obtains its food nutrients directly from the water or by an air mist sprayed directly onto the plant's roots.

Hydroponic gardening also requires the use of a growing media. Various mediums may be utilized which have to keep the roots abundantly moist. They need to also be in a position to support the plant's roots. These are the best media to date: enlarged clay, perlite, Styrofoam, lavender, rockwool, vermiculite, and pea gravel.

Many types plants which could be increased in a hydroponics system. Some plants will grow much better in a hydroponics system than many others, however, a number of the very popular are carrot, tomatoes, cucumbers, herbs, watercress, and also several other edible plants.

Tree seedlings and blossoms may also be grown using hydroponics. Hydroponic greenhouses are generating countless plant seedlings each year. These are subsequently transplanted and grown in other places where they're later planted into soil.

If you are only a beginner at hydroponic gardening, you may undoubtedly be more concerned with the level of your plants and the faster rate of expansion. Hydroponically grown plants will grow and grow faster and give you an earlier harvest of vegetable plants.

There are many advantages to growing your plants in a hydroponics system. Hydroponic gardening does not call for a fertile farmland or even a massive water source for growing crops. Vegetable and plants can be grown year-round. Hydroponic plants and vegetables can be grown in just about any small area, or a cellar, or even a flat balcony.

The hydroponic systems need less space since the plant's roots do not need to propagate and hunt for water and food. The smaller area requirement creates hydroponic gardening ideal for limited space house gardeners.

Hydroponic plants can likewise be grown in nurseries and greenhouses. The advantage of growing these crops with soil in a sterile medium comprises not needing to eliminate weeds or coping with soil-borne insects and diseases. And because most of the nutrients essential for the plant are easily accessible for this, the plant is more obviously fitter compared to plants grown in soil.

The best advantage to hydroponic gardening is your capacity to automate the hydroponics system with sockets and remote monitoring equipment. This lessens the time it requires to keep the crops and the growing air. Additionally, it enables the grower to leave their method for lengthy lengths of time without worrying about watering the plants.

Hydroponic growing without using soil isn't straightforward, but with time it will get to be very simple and regular. Hydroponics gives the benefit of several methods which may be beneficial to your crops and create a richer and healthy plant.

Hydroponics Versus Soil

To know exactly what the benefits are growing with hydroponics, first you need to know what hydroponics is. Hydroponics is straightforward. Hydroponics is growing with water rather than soil. Typically a person adds concentrated nutrients to the water, mimicking the fertilizers found in soil.

With hydroponics you have a great deal more control over your growth than you do with soil, because only adding the proper number of nutrients in the water ensures you will have the ideal quantity of food for your plants. In soil it can be more challenging to diagnose when you've little mineral trace elements, since you truly don't understand what exactly was missing to start with.

But when using hydroponics nutrients are pre-mixed with precisely the correct quantity of trace elements. Thus simply by adding the correct number of hydroponic nutrients into your own water from the hydroponic system, you are aware that the nutrients are blended properly and the crops have all of the components they need to survive. If your crops start to get sick like yellowing leaves because of a type of nutrient lack, all you need to do is ditch your hydroponic systems water, then fill it with fresh water and fresh nutrients.

In soil you'd need to look up the nutrient deficiencies in a book or manual to determine which sort of nutritional supplement is really missing or deficient. Either way it's possible to have a peek at the site homegrown-hydroponics.com below the tutorial section to get a nutrient discount calculator, which will show you exactly what plant afflicted deficiencies of particular types of plants will look like.

According to this guide you are able to make corrections. Hydroponics is easier as you can just nourish your hydroponics system and re-fill your hydroponics system using new water and new nutrients to repair the issue. This is significantly harder in soil.

Another massive benefit to hydroponics over soil is that in hydroponics it is possible to grow your plants up to ten times faster than in soil. In soil your crops need to come up with a very lengthy and very incorporated root system to receive all of the nutrients and water they require from the ground. Your plants will need to come up with a huge root system from the soil to be able to acquire everything that is vital for them to grow fast. Therefore, with a plant grown in soil you'd observe a huge root system below the ground, but a tiny plant above ground.

Hydroponics is precisely the contrary. As it's so it effortless for the crops to acquire the nutrients and water straight from the water in your reservoir, the plants can grow a lot smaller root system and also receive exactly the identical amount of nutrients, or more. With a hydroponic system you may expect to observe a plant with a tiny root system to get an extremely big plant above the ground. Fundamentally plants grow in hydroponics 10 times quicker versus soil growth. This is a massive benefit. Plants grown in hydroponics versus soil aren't just simpler to grow, but they grow much faster also.

Hydroponics is also very helpful for people who live in areas of the country with extreme environment conditions. People residing in a part of the country that's too hot, or too cold may make it rather hard to grow your crops. However, because hydroponics may be used inside you may control the temperature by employing either a heater or an air purifier.

Plants like to maintain a comfortable temperature exactly like individuals do. If you're able to keep your plants directly around 75 to 85° they'll grow like wildfire annually. It would not be possible to attempt to maintain these requirements outdoors, but it gets quite simple when using hydroponics. It's necessary for your plants not to get too hot or too cold during any portion of the entire year or you may stunt their growth.

Hydroponics makes it quick and easy for anybody in the world to readily grow their particular crops for food or for medicinal herbs. Hydroponics makes growing organics accessible to anyone with a supply of clean water and power. Hydroponics is being grown by NASA using the space station. One day our astronauts will probably be eating food grown from a hydroponic system, just like you're going to embark on.

Hydroponics basically provides your plants what they desire but in a spoon-fed fashion, which is a simple way of making them grow extremely fast. If you improve your hydroponic system by utilizing CO2, your crops can grow even twice that rate.

How is Hydroponic Gardening Different from Regular Gardening?

When growing via hydroponics, you will find a huge range of growing mediums which might be utilized. The mediums include substances such as perlite, vermiculite, coconut fiber, gravel, sand, or some variety of different substances. Even air might be utilized as a hydroponic growing medium. The hydroponic growing medium is notably an inert substance that doesn't provide any nourishment to the plants.

Each of the nutrition requirements comes in the nutrient solution, normally mixing fertilizer and water. Hydroponic fertilizer and fertilizer meant for usage in soil (regular fertilizer) include the three major nutrients. These nutrients are nitrogen, phosphorus, as well as potassium. The most important difference between hydroponic fertilizer and soil fertilizer is the fact that hydroponic gardening fertilizers include the appropriate amounts of each one of the vital micro-nutrients that fertilizers don't include. The crops are expected to discover these components in the soil.

Issues may arise for the plants if some or all the micro-nutrients aren't found in the soil or have been depleted by sequential or excess plantings. Hydroponic gardening fertilizers are often in a purer form compared to the regular fertilizers, so they're more secure and water-soluble.

Organic fertilizers are typically different than the hydroponic fertilizers or even the soil fertilizers in the way they deliver nourishment to plants. The organic fertilizers trust the action of microbes and bacteria to help divide the material into its fundamental elements so the plants can quickly use it. Hydroponic and regular fertilizers subsequently provide for the plants using these components.

Another difference between hydroponic and normal gardening is that growing hydroponics can be extremely complex. Hydroponics are controlled with sensors and computers that help control everything from watering cycles to nutrient power, and the total amount of light the plants receive. But hydroponics may also be rather straightforward. The normal home hydroponic system generally contains a couple of essential components, such as a growing menu, a reservoir, a timer controlled submersible pump to water the crops, along with an air pump to oxygenate the nutrient solution. Lighting is, of course, also needed to assist the hydroponic garden to grow.

Additionally, there are micro-nutrients which are needed for healthy plant growth. All these micro-nutrients include sulfur, calcium, magnesium, boron, cobalt, iron, copper, manganese, magnesium, and molybdenum.

These nutrients are the vital components plants need in tiny quantities.

Plants will probably become ill with no trace components and also will grow all kinds of issues if that nutrient is lost.

The lack of micro-nutrients in food plants can signify a deficiency of nutrition in the food. This is going to lead to the food not being as healthy as it might be and possibly lead folks to grow health issues as a result of deficiency of the vital elements. Any hydroponic gardener should use a good quality hydroponic fertilizer when they're growing plants with hydroponics.

It's also vital that the pH is regulated in both growing via hydroponics and in the soil. Plants lose the capability to consume unique nutrients once the pH varies. The pH needs to be monitored throughout the whole growth cycle of these plants to keep up the utmost healthy uptake of nutrients. The pH of the nutrient solution can influence how well each component can pass through the main cell wall to nourish the plant. When the gardener has correctly calibrated the proper concentrations and the pH of the solution, they can normally assume it'll remain steady barring any unexpected root disease.

Gardeners should always track their method too much instead of too little to prevent any issues. The ability to rapidly and easily examine and control pH in hydroponics is a significant benefit over regular gardening, where adjusting and testing the pH is considerably more complex and time consuming.

———

Advantages of Hydroponic Gardening

So, have you decided to grow a garden this season? Well, prior to going out and spending a great deal of money unnecessarily, you ought to have a peek at the benefits of hydroponic gardening. Hydroponic gardening is garden work at its very best. There's almost little to no soil involved with hydroponic growing. Hydroponic gardening is the usage of light and water to grow fruits and vegetables.

Hydroponic growing means less time and not as much money wasted on unnecessary substances. You don't have to spend money on pesticides and fertilizers. Nor would you spend hours weeding and tilling the ground. Hydroponic gardening is quite valuable because the yields on plants are much higher and the crops will normally generate richer, brighter, and more fruits.

To begin your personal hydroponic garden, you have to choose where you'll settle your crops. The hydroponic growth of crops generally implies that you need a nice quantity of room to enable the crops to grow. Many men and women use a greenhouse. Hydroponic growth of crops is quite straightforward and virtually everyone can get it done.

All you will need is to do just a bit of research, particularly if you're just beginning. Ask questions from those that you know who are in gardening. Learn what sort of nutrients that your plants will require. Hydroponic nutrients are often more concentrated due to the simple fact they have to get added into the plants and their growing environment. It's advisable if you discover a combination solution that will offer all the nutrients required for the plants to grow.

Another benefit to hydroponic gardening is you can grow your veggies and fruits throughout the year. The best situation is indoor hydroponic growing. This way it is possible to control not merely the water and light, but also the number of pests which will impact the return of these plants. When growing a garden outside, you need to be ready to eliminate some of your harvest yield as a result of pests, the weather, along with other aspects. But with hydroponic growing, you are able to remove the majority of these variables.

You might even be able to guarantee the quantity of hydroponic nutrients your plants need. By utilizing hydroponic nutrients, you can control the strength of their main systems and restrain the flowering potential of your crops. Various kinds of hydroponic nutrients may promote your plants to make more blossoms, which then provide more fruit in crops like the tomato plant. Other kinds of hydroponic nutrients boost the dimensions and foliage of these plants. Hydroponic nutrients are essentially plant food. This is as vital to the plant's growth as light and water.

We understand that you will find three or more items that are indispensable to hydroponic gardening: light, water, and hydroponic nutrients. Without those three things, your hydroponic garden will certainly fail.

Learn more about the essentials of hydroponic growing to make sure you get a fantastic year-round garden.

You won't regret it once you find the bountiful harvest at the end of the road.

5 Environmental Advantages of Hydroponics

1. Less Land Is Needed

Among the best things about hydroponics is that less land is required to grow crops, in comparison with conventional farming techniques.

By way of example, if you are planting rows upon rows of lettuce, cabbage or tomato plants in soil, you're consuming a great deal of space.

Regrettably, there's a limited amount of space and appropriate farmland on Earth.
With conventional farming, you may be as streamlined as you would like, however it remains true that each plant you put in the ground occupies a predetermined space that does not change during the maturation period of the plant.

This is different when you are using hydroponics. Grow pots can be put closer together, without causing any issues in the growth rate of the plants. Nutrients from the growing way are distributed differently in water in comparison with soil.

—

Actually, industrial hydroponics have a tendency to absorb just 1/5 of the land necessary for the exact same number of plants being cultivated on farmland.

If you are wondering how hydroponics farmers conserve a lot of land, one way is by building systems in a manner so a number of the plants can be suspended in mid-air to conserve space.

A grower can additionally use numerous levels of glass with appropriate plumbing to make exactly the identical impact in their plants.

The main point?

With only a little land, you can achieve a great deal with hydroponics. With commercial hydroponic farming, there's less of a need to strip the surroundings (such as forests) for farmland.

2. Reduced Fossil Fuel Use with Adaptive Growing Spots

This may not seem like an environmental advantage, but it is. Just imagine how much fuel do we use on a daily basis to send food long distances to markets?

With hydroponics, commercial growers have the choice of setting their greenhouses in places which are closer to their intended markets or distribution channels.

Basically, this cuts the need for costly transport. This boosts the benefit of this hydroponics grower and cuts the contamination linked to the transport of products.

And while this may not look like a major deal, the combined impact of several hydroponics growers over the years does make a difference.

Think about things from the long-term. The flexibility of hydroponics aids the environment by decreasing emissions and the general carbon footprint connected with food production and promotes transportation.

3. Less Water is Used

Evidently, water consumption is something which most of us consider if we are nurturing plants.

Crops will need to be constantly hydrated, and they'll readily dry out if there is not sufficient watering. The issue with soil is that when the water is put on, it's consumed by the soil and also the surplus sinks beyond the roots.

Therefore, we must continually replenish the source of water to keep plants alive and hydrated.

With hydroponics, there is a fundamental nutrient reservoir or water bank, and the water in this water bank is circulated or sent directly into the crops.

There's some reduction to evaporation, which can be ordinary, but a lot of this water is kept for weeks and days.

For the most part, Hydroponics systems are preserved by adding nutrients into the water. There's not any need to pump fresh water into the system.

In reality, hydroponic growing uses just 10 percent of the water that would be necessary to grow plants in conventional soil. Just imagine how much water can be saved over long intervals!

4. Potentially Better for The Earth and Soil

Soil erosion is simply among the issues related to traditional farming.

In some countries, older forests, that are a part of the Earth's "lungs," are cut down and cleared to turn large areas into agricultural soil.

The quantity of farmable land available for industrial agriculture has been steadily decreasing because of the Second World War.

Land is now so rare that we're touching nature's reserves of forests, only so we can keep on growing food to support the Earth's ever-growing human population.

Obviously, you will still need just a little bit of land when you participate in hydroponics.

However, unlike conventional farming, the total amount of land required for hydroponics is radically decreased. So much more could be carried out with hydroponics in a little space, when compared with conventional farming.

And, because it doesn't require soil, hydroponic growing clinics may be utilized in regions with harsh weather and little fertile soil, such as in the desert.

Furthermore, there are various sorts of hydroponics setups. You can blend hydroponics and aquaculture and think of an aquaponics system which creates not only vegetables, fruits, and flowers, but also fish.

The quantity of time needed to grow a number of batches of crops is the exact same time necessary for fish to grow to plate-size.

Just imagine the benefits of employing hydroponics for commercial-scale farming of vegetables, fruits and other plants.

5. Reduced Utilization of Pesticides and Herbicides

In traditional farming, 2 types of sprays are employed: pesticides and herbicides.

Herbicides are sprayed to eliminate undesirable plants (these are normally known as weeds), whereas pesticides have been employed to control pest insects.

The spraying of pesticides and herbicides do a lot of damage to the surroundings:

Pesticides could be swept off by rain, contaminating nearby ecosystems. And, pesticides do not just poison the insect, but may possibly poison other creatures too.

But with hydroponics, there's absolutely no weed growth since it takes some time for crops to grow in a hydroponic grow medium. Hydroponic grow medium doesn't function just like soil. There is absolutely no requirement to use herbicides.

There also is not much need for pesticide usage. Why?

For the most part, crops will be guarded by closed greenhouses. These greenhouses may be reinforced to withstand insect pest strikes.

Less use of pesticides and herbicides is great for the environment since this may mean radically reduced runoff, which influences both the soil and bodies of water.

Among the looming problems which has influenced us is pesticide runoff. Pesticide molecules are discovered in the meat of fish and other animals, which signifies the runoff from agricultural lands is now so prevalent that it's invaded creatures and lands that it should not be found in.

Types of Hydroponic System

Plant foliage necessitates light, oxygen and carbon dioxide. Plant root systems demand water, oxygen and nutrients. When crops are grown generally water sucks up nutrients in the soil and carries them into the roots. The nutrients and water are consumed by the roots to nourish plant development. Soil drainage subsequently enables water to be substituted by air in the openings between soil grains. This provides the roots with oxygen.

In hydroponics the nutrients are dissolved in water. Soil is substituted with a growing medium to provide the roots with oxygen, oxygen and nutrients. Hydro juice (nutrient solution) could be pumped to every plant, it may also be employed to frequently flood the main room, then drain out. Both approaches need a timer and pump to circulate the nutrients through the roots and therefore, are covered with these notes and diagrams.

Roots is also increased from the air by spraying blossoms using a fine mist of hydro juice, or increased at the hydro juice and also the solution aerated beneath every root mass using an air pump. With the next two approaches that the plants must fastened at the bottom of the stem or something.

The hydroponic system described does the work and is acceptable for practically any plant using stringy roots. I haven't tried it using almost any bulb plants or crops like orchids that need fungus or mold in the soil to grow.

This system is comparable to Nutrient Film Technique (NFT) the lean Rockwool slit and behaves like a capillary mat. This removes the requirement to have a horizontal bottom on the main room and also to level the base of root room, making it simpler and cheaper to install. This method will find the most vigorous expansion if every plant gets its own needs via a drip feed.

The dripper is positioned so it trickles onto the roots growing at the bottom of the seedling block, and the roots will grow thick, hairy and streamlined under the dripper. A 4L each hour dripper is utilized, nevertheless their drip speed depends upon pressure, this can be affected by size and height of the drip feed container. The trickle rate will slow as the tank empties.

Feeding may also be accomplished with a quicker dripper near the peak of each leading end of every side of the main room. The crops grown similar to this had a huge root mass, the roots of the plant taking around a third of the main room.

With the timer I could just flood the main room every four hours, and the growth rate was comparable to the past. The expansion rate will improve by flooding it every hour or less. Following that the root room is bombarded and it must drain into a trickle in a couple of minutes.

Starting Plants

Wipe seeds in moist newspaper or cotton wool, cover seeds using moist paper or fabric, drain off surplus water and do not allow to dry out. After the seed root is two - 5mm long put the seed root in the little hole with tweezers. Be certain the root is shielded from the open branches of the tweezers and the root or seed is not squashed. Then put the seedling block up hole onto a plate and add moist Rockwool till it will not require any more water.

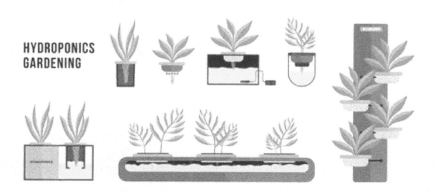

HYDROPONICS GARDENING

Maintain the plate on an angle for drainage, however, the seedling cubes should not dry out a lot and seedling should appear in a couple of days. Seedlings can remain on the plate till roots grow out of the base or sides of this seedling block. While this occurs, seedling is all set to be transplanted to the Rockwool mat in the main room. (Ahead of the seedling cubes going in the main room the rockwool is soaked in warm water 24 hours, and then afterward with hydro juice at half power.) Roots will grow from the seedling block, through and across to the other side of the Rockwool mats.

Put three to eight plants on each side, evenly dispersed across the system slots, and it'll soon grow into a bulk of green. After the system is usable and plants are growing, the interior of the main room will have a rich earthy odor. There will be three or four crops in case you're growing them large (outside), eight in case your growing quickly and flowering early (under lights).

If the roots grow up in the base or sides of the Rockwool block it is time to transplant to the tube. After the roots have grown to the mat, you can also reach them with full power of the hydro juice. Light proof plastic ought to be utilized to disburse over the surface of the main room as this will be to prevent green slime from growing on the rockwool. This can only be achieved when the plant is tall, so be careful not to strain or harm the plants.

Many seeds need special requirements to germinate. By way of instance, many garden vegetables and herb seeds will need to stay moist or wet for a while. Seeds can be germinated in a hydroponic grower, and frequently they germinate better than in soil.

Planting Seeds

Most seeds have been put under the surface of the media. A proposed positioning is from 1/2 into 1 inch under the surface. This keeps the seeds quite moist and provides it some sense for where the lighting is and where the dark is. The root of this plant will grow towards the dark and the water, along with the plant leaves and stem will proceed towards the light.

Many seed packs include directions for soil and mention just how deep to bury the seeds. They may be implanted at precisely the exact same thickness in hydroponics. Some seeds, such as corn and beans, will germinate in only a couple of days. Some others, like tomato, bell pepper and herbs can take as long as fourteen days till they appear. Growers with seeds must be watered every day, even if no crops are seen. If you don't find any indication of life after fourteen days, it's ideal to replant the grower. Sometimes the grower root place will be quite so cold or so tender, the seeds won't germinate.

To germinate tiny seeds such as many types of flowers, a distinctive kind of germination could be deemed necessary. 1 method is to begin the seeds between 2 pieces of paper or a towel saturated with water. The towel is kept moist daily. Germinating some kinds of seeds is much more complex than simply soaking them in water. Some seeds will need to get broken in some manner to germinate, and many others are specialized and respond to intervals of light or temperature. If there's something you need to increase, it may be helpful to understand what the seed demands are so they will germinate.

The Principal Methods of Regrowth

Some crops can reproduce from cuttings. This usually means cutting a little portion of the growing tip of a plant, pulling off the ground leaves and adhering the cut end into the growing media. A few of the crops which may be replicated from cuttings are basil and a number of the other herbs.

Garlic reproduces from individual garlic cloves. Some of the garlic at the supermarket is treated and won't sprout. A natural garlic is much more likely to sprout.

Potatoes are grown from a planted potato. The potato may be cut into bits or planted whole.

Root Chamber

The root chamber is produced from 90mm. PVC storm water pipe, which is the kind used for new building construction. Fittings are available in large hardware stores. Fittings incorporate appropriate angles, tee junctions, end caps and many other pieces. These may be utilized to produce the main chamber to suit any space. The main camber is created with two spans around 1 meter for the sides, 2 spans roughly of 600mm for the endings and 4 right angles to the corners. PVC pipe adhesive is utilized to attach each of them and make them water tight.

A slot is cut from the top of every side to provide access to alter growing medium and eliminate root mass. Holes rather than a slot could be used for every single plant, so yet another method of accessibility has to be utilized. A drain hole or holes have to be drilled at the base of one end of the main pipe and a flooding hole is drilled at front of the opposite end. The main system is mounted at an angle with the drain end below, then the flooding end. This is to make certain the roots do not get water logged. Too much of the angle will create the Rockwell and roots to dry out in the top end.

Flood and Drain

A flood and drain system need a timer, a pump and a drain tank to grab the hydro juice. A hose is run by the base of the drain tank into the pump inlet.

A hose is run out of the pump outlet to the hole at the cover of the flooding (large) end of the main system. The pump inlet is beneath the underside the drain tank.

When the drain tank is filling hydro juice flows through the pump inlet through the pump and then upwards to the flooding hose at an angle with the hydro juice from the tank. This will be to prime the pump since the pump cannot suck air, it may only push what leaks from the inlet.

The timer runs on the pump for 1 minute and the hydro juice fills about half of the root system. If the system overflows the grow size of the drain holes. When a hose is used at the end, it should not trigger the hydro juice to settle in the drain end. A recycling bin is excellent for the drain tank (see end of Drip Feed section to attach hose to empty tank). When putting the pump onto the ground along with the drain tank bricks you must lift it and prime the pump.

Ebb and Flow (Flood and Drain)

The Ebb and Flow system functions by temporarily flooding the grow tray with nutrient solution and then draining the solution back into the reservoir. This activity is normally done using a submerged pump that's linked to a timer. After the timer turns on the pump nutrient solution is pumped to the growing tray. After the timer shuts off the pump the nutrient solution flows back to the reservoir. The timer is set to come on a few times each day, based on the size and kind of plants, humidity and temperature and the kind of growing medium utilized.

The Ebb and Flow is a useful system which could be utilized with a number of growing mediums. The complete grow menu could be full of Grow Rocks, gravel or granular Rockwool. Lots of people like to utilize individual pots full of growing medium, this makes it a lot easier to move plants around or perhaps transfer them out of the system. The most important disadvantage of the kind of system is that with a few kinds of growing medium (Gravel, Grow rocks, Perlite), there's a vulnerability to power outages in addition to timer and pump failures. The roots may dry out immediately when the watering cycles are disrupted. This issue may be alleviated somewhat by utilizing growing media that keeps in more water (Rockwool, Vermiculite, coconut fiber or some fantastic soilless mixture like Pro-mix or even Faffard's).

DWC (Deep Water Staff)

The articulation "DWC" is every now and used incorrectly when depicting water civilization constructions. So what's "DWC," and for what reason is "DWC" not among the six kinds of hydroponic constructions? Everything considered, that's in light of how it is just not a replacement kind of hydroponic construction in any manner shape or form. As should be apparent from the entire title "Heavy Water Staff," it is only an assortment of this ahead of an existing type of semi-automatic system referred to as a water civilization arrangement. "Deep" facing is possibly utilized to depict a few water culture systems once the water value in the construction is greater than 8-10 inches, so then it will generally be described as a real DWC system. At any rate paying small character into the water value, DWC systems remain water civilization constructions.

As a rule the water/supplement plan of action significance should not be greater than just 8 inches. That's incredibly necessary for larger plants which have higher root structures which require more room, as well as more water.

Or on the flip side whilst utilizing a compartment such as a can that should be filled satisfactorily high to cover the plant's crucial root ball close to the top satisfactorily.

Plants such as the magnitude of the majority of groupings of lettuce may without a small stretch be made using just 4-6 drops of water from the water culture methods.

No matter what is what believed, there is no distinction between how a normal water culture system and a DWC (heavy water civilization) construction works or restricts. The correct thought is that the principle distinction between both is the importance of the water from the computer system. Despite if it is a normal water culture strategy, a true DWC construction, or one that reuses a regular water system or actual DWC construction, regardless of everything you need to ensure you have sufficient water quantity, and amazing oxygenation into the origin structure to encourage the crops.

Water volume is not exactly equal to water importance. Should you choose a gallon of water and then put it into a broad bay, the water level may just be an inch or two large, however you can put a relative gallon of water into a three inch wide area, the water elevation will be progressively like two feet. So water quantity and importance are two completely different things.

Should the water level be over or beneath the receptacles?

There is normally chaos and sometimes perhaps a chat which water/supplement system ought to be used to maintain water culture constructions. What if the basket gets into the water hanging essentially over it? There are upsides and pitfalls for the two, anyhow there's not anything unchangeable, as it can generally be. The water amount is similarly rapidly and simple to modify in a water culture arrangement by essentially including additional water, or taking some out.

Right after the air pockets soil in the elevated intention of the water, then they fly to the water's surface. At the stage when they pop, they scatter unassuming small water dots an inch or two on the water's surface. The grade of those tiny water dots gets sprinkled around depends upon, how much air is actually being presented, and therefore, the amount of air pockets is slowly scaling into the surface via the air stones.

Right after the receptacle is not hitting onto the water and dangling just above it, then those little sprinkling water dots keep the growing media close to the bottom of the pockets soaked. How tacky it is dependent upon exactly what amount of air flow you have and that is scattering about the water surface close to the instance.

A decent relationship is standing it out from bubbling water (overpowering moving heating up, a shifting air pocket, transports, essentially bubbling).

—

Getting a moving air pocket perfect, and basically bubbling is important. Another variable is the sort of growing media which is used. Some growing media will maintain moisture faster and simpler than many others, which is going to have a considerable effect also.

Right if the receptacles are hitting the air, the growing media in the containers may hold/wick more water than when they had been hanging over it, also this really is a section of the time more valuable. Whatever the case, the type of growing media will have substantial impact since a few growing systems will absorb and maintain moistness quicker and simpler than others. Along these lines it may wind up being completely water logged close to the bottom of these compartments if it is in contact with water. If it does, simply decrease the water level so the baskets are hanging over the water instead, or utilize an alternative type of growing media.

It is in a like fashion simple to indicate how immense the plant has any type of effect too. The plants roots are going to ignore the water/supplement match program. Which implies they'll go, and grow wherever it has proper moisture.
In the event the plant is almost nothing and the origins have not been outside the bottom of this compartment nonetheless, it might be important to keep the bushels from touching water.

In any event before the follicles are turning out to stand outside the foundation and lengthy enough to stay submerged.

In any event, once the bottom of these cartons is beautiful and saturated by a whole lot of unassuming water dots sprinkling round by the popping up air bubbles while dangling across the water. The excess moisture near the plant's crucial root ball in the growing media actually brightens up the water/supplement plan of activity while the cartons hitting the water may accelerate root progress, whereas the crops and root mass are pretty much anything.

Drip Feed System.

This feed system includes a dripper for every plant. Dripping the hydro juice right on the cover of the main mass must block the plant by sending out long roots seeking food. Resulting in more expansion on top or so the theory goes. The drip method uses a drip tank roughly one meter over the drippers and reticulation system. Reticulation is through 13mm. Poly tubing to just over the main system. A hole is punched in the 13mm. tube. A 4mm. jack is inserted into the hole. Subsequently 4mm. poly tubing is connected to the 4mm. adapter. A dripper is connected to the opposite end of this 4mm. tube. The 4mm poly tubing ought to be kept as brief as possible so there's sufficient pressure to begin the drippers.

Barbed right angles and tee shirt are utilized to track the 13mm poly tubes near every plant. The top of this 13 mm. poly tubing is about 50mm. Beneath the base of the drip tank a 13mm. Into Snap-On adapter is fitted into the peak of this 13mm. poly tube. The 13 mm. poly tubing is set at right angles into the slot along with the 4mm. adapter, 4 mm. Poly tubing along with the dripper is placed over the slots in the system. Any leakage in the mix at the poly tubing will trickle in the slot, preventing reduction of hydro juice. A 42 liter plastic garbage container and lid is utilized for the drip tank. Snap-on fittings and 13mm. garden hose link the base of the drip container into the to 13mm. poly tube. They also link the pump outlet hose into the peak of the drip tank.

A cease Snap-on is utilized where the garden hose connects to the Snap-on adapter on the 13mm. poly tube. This averts the hydro juice from flowing out once the Snap-on is eliminated from your 13mm. poly tube. To convert from drain and flood to trickle feed transfer the pump outlet hose out of the flooding inlet on top of the main room, to the top of the drip tank. Snap-on universal sprinkler adapter are utilized to connect hoses into both sides of the drip feed container.

All these really are a Snap-on to 13 mm thread adapter. There's also a 20 mm. thread that screws onto a 13 mm. thread. A hole no bigger than 13 mm ribbon is drilled into the face of the tank. The 13 mm ribbon is pushed through the hole in the exterior of the tank. Currently the 20 mm. ribbon is screwed onto the 13 mm ribbon within the tank producing a watertight seal. Be sure the hole is off from impediments within the tank which would stop the 20 mm. ribbon from attaching to the 13 mm. thread. This way is used for all tanks and additionally for the pump outlet hose link to the top of the flooding end of the main system.

Drip Systems Recovery / Nonrecovery

Drip systems are possibly the most frequently used form of hydroponic system on Earth. Operation is straightforward, a timer controls a submersed pump. The timer turns the pump on and nutrient solution is dripped on the bottom of each plant with a little drip point. In a Retrieval Drip System the surplus nutrient solution that runs off is accumulated in the reservoir to get re-used.

The Non-Recovery System doesn't collect off the run.

A restoration system employs nutrient solution a little better, as excessive solution is reused, this also allows for the usage of a cheaper timer as a restoration system does not need exact control of the watering cycles.

The non-recovery system ought to have a more exact timer so that watering cycles could be adjusted to assure that the plants have enough nutrient solution along with the runoff is kept to a minimal.

The non-recovery system requires less maintenance because of how the surplus nutrient solution is not recycled back into the reservoir, therefore the nutrient potency and pH of this reservoir won't change. This usually means you could fill the reservoir with pH adjusted nutrient solution then forget it till you need to mix more. A restoration system may have substantial changes in the pH and nutrient power levels that need regular checking and correcting.

Water Culture System

Convert an aquarium to an easy hydroponic system. The crops have been suspended over a floating Styrofoam platform. This system is a favorite for classrooms since the roots of these plants are observable hanging beneath the floating platform.

Materials Required:

Aquarium - Any watertight container with slightly vertical sides will get the job done. Light breaks down the nutrient solution and also promotes algae growth, therefore if you use an aquarium, you'll have to build a light shield from cardboard or aluminum foil to keep light from the reservoir (shrub). Should you like to observe the roots make the light protector (or a part of it) detachable.

Floating Platform - You'll require a sheet of Styrofoam 1 1/2" to 2" thick. Cut Styrofoam to fit loosely within the aquarium (or whatever you're using for a reservoir).

Plastic Cups - Use a few small plastic or Styrofoam cups to keep the plants around the floating stage. (NOTE: We typically use Solo brand 3oz. Plastic bathroom cups, however, you may use any little plastic cup so long as it has tapered sides).

Growing Medium - You'll require a small quantity of growing medium, sufficient to fill the plastic cups.

Air Pump and Air Stone - It is necessary to use an air pump and air stone to oxygenate the nutrient solution. A normal air pump used for an aquarium is all that's necessary.

Hydroponic Fertilizer - A fantastic quality hydroponic fertilizer is necessary, regular "soil" fertilizers do not include essential "micro-nutrients."

pH Test Kit - You may need some method of assessing and adjusting the pH of your nutrient solution.

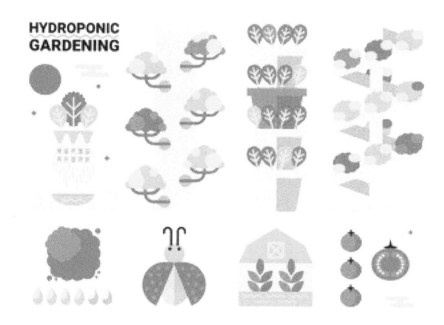

HYDROPONIC GARDENING

Assembly of System:

1. Cut the Styrofoam float to match the reservoir. Cut the float somewhat smaller than the opening so it will not bind up as soon as the water level varies.

2. Cut the holes at the Float into the suitable size to your plastic cups you're using, you would like the bottoms of the cups to hang below the base of the float but not collapse through. (NOTE: We typically use Solo brand 3oz. Plastic bathroom cups, these need a 1 7/8" to two" hole.

3. Cut several holes (approx... 1/8" into 1/4" dia.) At the base of your plastic cups. Add growing medium to the cup (NOTE: when the growing medium drops out through the holes, you'll be able to set a little piece of fiberglass screen or little bit of fabric over the holes prior to adding the growing medium.

4. Plant your seedling, Rooted cutting or seed in the growing medium.

Care and Feeding Instructions

1. Fill the aquarium (reservoir) with water. Mix your nutrient solution according to the guides on the fertilizer package. Check pH and adjust accordingly. NB: The mandatory pH value will be different based upon the necessities of the plant.

2. Attach 1/4" air line into the air stone and put the air stone in the window. Twist free the end of tubing to air stone and then plug in the air stone into the socket, be certain there are bubbles coming out of the air stone.

(NOTE: NEVER submerge the air conditioner in water as electric shock could happen).

3. Place the floating platform in addition to the nutrient solution. Put plastic cups with the holes at the floating stage.

4. When the crops have used up roughly half of this nutrient solution it is possible to include WATER ONLY to bring the level back up (don't include fertilizer or you might give rise to a nutrient build up which could damage the crops). Recheck pH and adjust if needed.

5. When the crops have utilized half the nutrient solution, the next time you need to replace the nutrient solution by draining the reservoir and mixing a fresh batch. Utilize the old nutrient solution on house plants or other plants.

Windowsill Wonder.

Anyone can build an easy, automated system without having to spend a great deal of cash. This system is well suited to fit in a kitchen windowsill--even though it may easily Be enlarged to accommodate any growing plant set.

Each of the substances required for this system are available at discount superstores, aquarium supply shops, or hardware stores for under $25.

We utilized a 2-liter jar for the nutrient reservoir and also an ice cube tray for the plant trough. After you understand the logistics, feel free to experiment with different containers. To prepare your nutrient reservoir, then drill two holes in the cap of this 2-liter bottle.

The holes must be Just large enough to snugly hold the 1/4-inch tube directly through the connectors. 1 hole is going to be to for your water and another will be on your airline. Drill a hole at the side of this trough (the ice cube tray) as near the bottom as you can. If you intend on enlarging your system, then drill a second hole on the other side.

Insert it directly through straps in the drilled holes. Produce an excellent seal round the straps with adhesive or silicon caulk. Create your own water supply hose by drilling a few smallish holes in a piece of irrigation tube cut to match the base of the trough. Connect 1 end of the tube into one of the fixtures onto the inside of the trough. The opposite end of this tube may be sealed using a dab of adhesive or caulk.

If you plan on growing your system, do not seal the opposite end. Rather, join it to another fitting on the other side of this trough. Connect the water from the nutrient reservoir into the trough.

Cut a second piece to precisely the exact same size as the nutrient reservoir. Then join this on the other side of this water line connector, on the inside of the bottle cap. The line must hang down to the base of the 2-liter bottle once the cap is still on. Run the air in the air pump into another directly through the connector over the cap of the bottle. At a certain stage in the air, splice the line to spend the hands. Away from the T, join the airline valve.

Fill your 2-liter bottle with water till it is about three-quarters full. Reconnect it to a trough and set the trough where it's going to be located. Turn on the air pump and close the valve. The water is going to be pushed to the trough. Gently ease open the valve so the water is slowly moving to the trough really gradually. It's fine when it takes up to a half hour to get the air pump to push all of the water from the bottle. The purpose here would be to get the valve shut enough to permit sufficient pressure to build in the bottle to push out the water, but open enough to allow air to escape if the pump is away, so the water may flow back in the bottle.

Now you are ready to include the medium and plants. We discovered that heated clay or lava stone works well. Any range of plants will operate within this particular system. Succulent herbs, like peppermint and ginger, are especially easy to grow.

If you would like to broaden your system, just construct another trough and attach the water line of this new trough at the end of the last trough. We discovered that up to 2 modules of this size can be powered by precisely the exact same pump and nutritional supplement bottle. Flooding and draining the machine one time each day ought to be adequate. But if you are growing a massive amount of plants in a sunny place, you might need to flood and drain the system two times daily.

The "Aquafarm"

This system was grown and popularized by General Hydroponics almost two decades back as their first item. The initial layout, which remains in creation, is called the "Aquafarm." In the past few years it has seen new embodiments called the "Water garden" (a decorative variant), the "Power grower" (a revised version of this water garden), the "Water farm" (a square variant), and also the "Megafarm" (a 20 gallon variation).

An identical bucket established system is also being marketed by another company under the name of this "Universal Garden."

These units are very reliable, simple to operate and are extremely straightforward to construct. Everyone these systems retail for 50 dollars for each unit array.

This record will demonstrate how you can create this kind of system for a low price. This system will accommodate several tiny plants (as well suited to) or hold one big plant. Personally, I have noticed a 12 foot tall tree being grown within an aquafarm, in addition to a huge banana tree, both inside.

The crops have been grown in a room suspended over a reservoir (essentially a bucket in a container) that retains the nutrient solution. A small aquarium pump forces an easy pumping mechanism that provides nourishment from the reservoir near the top of the growing system, in which it trickles down through the root canal and to the reservoir. This system is so powerful it isn't unusual for tomato crops to grow more than 4 inches every day! This system gives tremendous yields!

Assembly Directions

1. Remove the grips in the buckets.

2. Drill drainage holes at the base of the 3.5 gallon bucket. The size of the drainage holes isn't crucial, keep them small enough to keep your growing medium from falling into the nutrient reservoir. I typically drill holes someplace around 5/32" in diameter. Furthermore, make certain to drill holes to get sufficient drainage. I typically drill roughly 30 to 40 holes in a pattern much like the one pictured to the right.

3. Drill the pump column hole at the base of the 3.5 gallon bucket. Utilize a 13/16" diameter spade drill bit to achieve this. Drill this hole about two inches from the outer edge of the bucket. Check with the drawing for positioning.

Eventually, when drilling the hole move with mild pressure and, even in case you've got a variable speed drill, then a slow drill rate. Prepare yourself to stop the drill when you break through the skillet, should you continue to drill as soon as you've pierced the bucket, then the piece will rattle from the pit and "hog" out it into a bigger, triangular shaped pit. A complete hole at the 5 gallon bucket is vital for the grommet to seal correctly, so it is worth it to practice here where it actually doesn't count.

4. Drill the grommet hole in the face of the five toasters. Drill this hole in the face of the bucket as near the ground as you can. Take care not to pierce the base web of this bucket. Unfortunately, I cannot provide you the precise size of this hole to drill since there are numerous kinds of rubber grommets that change slightly in size. You'll have to quantify your grommet and ascertain what size hole to drill (that ought to be in the ballpark of 3/4" or 13/16"). I recommend you drill a test hole in something apart from your bucket and examine the match of this grommet. The diagram at right shows the 5 gallon bucket with the hole drilled, the rubber grommet fitted along with also the elbow pressed into position.

5. Insert the rubber grommet into the 5 gallon bucket. It's necessary that the grommet creates a watertight seal with the bucket, which means you might need to remove any burrs left in the drilling process using a knife.

6. Add the elbow to the rubber grommet. When you push on the elbow to the grommet grip your hands on the grommets' back side to keep it from pushing into the bucket. Add the elbow around halfway to the grommet so there is still space to swivel. When you are done with this thing you need to have something which resembles the drawing.

7. Attach the 10" long, 1/2" I.D. tube into the elbow. Attach this tube to the section of the elbow on the surface of the bucket. This tube will work to indicate the degree of nutrient in the Aquafarm. When it is time to alter the solution it also serves as a drain, then you merely swivel down it and allow the solution to drain out!

8. Insert the 3.5 gallon bucket into the 5 gallon bucket. Now you've finished the body of this Aquafarm and you ought to have something which resembles the drawing.

9. Cut the pump column support tube. After the diagram, cut the 1/2" pvc pipe into 14" in length measuring from the tip of the bevel. Make the cut at roughly 45 degrees.

10. Add the pump column support tubing (from previous step) into its hole (from step 3) at the base of the 3.5 gallon bucket. Add it beveled first and then push it all of the way in, till it bottoms out from the nutrient reservoir.

11. Cut the tee shown. A little hacksaw works best. Discard both little pieces.

12. Cut and drill the drip ring. Cut the 5/16" O.D. tubing to 15 inches and drill seven 1/8" diameter holes evenly spaced along its length (refer to the diagrams below).

13. Add the drip ring to the "tee." Place the ends of the tube into the cut ends of this "tee." Ensure that the holes in the tube point to the stem of the "tee." Set this aside for later.

14. Heating the 3/16" Aquarium tubing. Heat the tube around 1" from the end before it's soft enough to bend. Rotate it only on the tip of a fire so it's evenly heated, only a couple seconds will do just fine.

15. Bend the tube. Make the bend to a little less than 45 degrees. It's necessary that you don't kink the tube as air has to flow through it.

16. Reduce the tube. Bevel the end of the tube as shown. The period of the bent part of the tube should be approximately 1/4" long.

17. Drill the hole in the 3/8" O.D. pump tube. Drill a 3/16" diameter hole at the side of the pump column tube, roughly 1 inch from the end.

18. Build the pump column. Add the bent end of this 3/16" volcano tubing to the hole at the pump tube. Seal the joint using a non-water resistant adhesive. Hot glue is fantastic, but something such as sandpaper works also. Place paste the aquarium tube into the pump tube in many areas also.

19. Attach the pump column into the drip ring. Slip the drip ring above the pump column, so do not paste it. Voila! You have finished the pump column!

20. Last measure. Add the pump column gathering to the pvc service tube. You should now have something similar to the drawing beneath. Congratulations on finishing your initial "aquafarm."

Nutrient Film Technique

The N.F.T. method (Nutrient Film Technique) is pervasive with home hydroponic cultivators too. Overwhelmingly by virtue of its own clear structure. In any instance N.F.T. systems are usually acceptable for, and many frequently employed for growing smaller actively growing plants such as different kinds of lettuce. Next to growing lettuce, some company manufacturers also produce various kinds of blossoms and greens utilizing N.F.T. systems.

Even though you will find a range of ways to plan a N.F.T. program, all of them have a relative standard for an exceedingly shallow improvement plan of activity falling through the tube. Where the found fundamental institutions of these plants collaborate with all the water, and will hold the improvements out of it. The notable drawback to some N.F.T. process is that the crops are sensitive to fractures in the motion of water from electricity outages (or some other reason). The plants will start to shrivel fast at whatever stage the water ceases traveling through the system.

What you need to make a N.F.T. system:

• Container to maintain the growing system (like a vault)
• Submersible fountain/lake siphon

• Tubing to maneuver water directly into the N.F.T. growing chambers

• Growing tubes for the plants to grow in (also referred to as a gap/channel)

• Beginner squares, or small baskets and growing media to begin afresh

• Yield arrangement (tube, stations) to take care of the growing system back to the store

How a hydroponic N.F.T. structure works is actually crucial. Supplement game program is steered up from the shop, when compared with to some mind boggling that spouses the increased tubing to various ones that are smaller. Each of these smaller chambers conducts supplement response for a single side of each of the growing channels/crevasse's together with the plants inside. A dainty layer (film) of this enhancement game program courses through each of the redirect's using the plants inside to the other hand, passing by every plant and shake the origins on the bottom of the station as it will. The improvement plan of action flows starting with a single side then on another considering the manner in which the station is slanted so the water flows downhill.

The plants from the growing chambers (channel/gorge) are usually suspended within the water by placing seedlings started in beginner squares or a minimum one-fifth of growing media into small openings at the most notable intention of the room.

The organizations of this seedlings hang down to the bottom of this chamber/channel where they get nutritional supplements via the supplement plan gushing by. The plenitude supplement plan of action flows from this very low end of every one the stations into a different channel or room, and is directed back to the shop where it's reused via the growing system.

Even though the growing solution coursing through the stations is remarkably shallow, the all the plants main mass stays moist by the roots using a wick to soak up water apparently of these origins, just like through moisture that's stored within the chamber/channel. The roots which are hung between the bottom of the plant and the water level from the station have sogginess for to, however again can get enough oxygen in the air enveloping them within the chamber/channel as well.

Business growers customarily utilize uncommonly made channels/crevasses to get N.F.T. systems which have flat bottoms with indents conducting the lengthy route along the station. These holes enable water to flow underneath the main mass and help protect it in pooling or damming up.

Home growers a lot of the time use a vinyl deluge waterway for their stations. These vinyl spouts have comparative sections, and are moderately priced.

Home growers also often use an ADS (Advanced Drainage System) water frame tubing for N.F.T. constructions. The ADS tubing does not have grooves, however by increasing the incline to inspection, the curved tube works well also.

Aeroponics

Even though the possibilities of this aeroponic structure is extremely clear, it is really the most special of all the kinds of hydroponic systems. At any rate it is still truly simple to construct your own one of a type of essential aeroponic system, and a great deal of home growers like growing plants in them too, as well as get outstanding results utilizing this sort of hydroponic construction.

Like with another sort of hydroponic system, you may use a broad range of types of materials to fabricate it, likewise as a broad range of sorts of construction system strategies to fit into your area. You are really only confined by the room you have, along with your integrity that is innovative.

A few focal points to utilizing an aeroponic systems are that they customarily use no growing media. The roots get the most significant oxygen, and also the plants build up much more quickly in such a fashion.

Aeroponic systems also use less water than other types of semi-automatic structures (particularly aeroponic systems). Additionally, harvesting is commonly simpler, particularly for root plants.

At any rate there are a couple drawbacks to aeroponic structures also. Apart from being the more costly to make, the sprinkler heads may clog from work of this split up mineral components from the growing plan of action. So, try to have additional things nearby to swap out whenever they do obstruct as you wash them.

Additionally, thinking about the manner the developing plants are hanging by construction in aeroponic techniques, the plants roots are even more vulnerable to drying out when there is a break in the watering cycle. Thusly, any electrical outage (in any capacity at all) can make your crops die significantly more quickly than another sort of hydroponic system. In like fashion there is a diminished advantage for screw up with the improvement amounts in aeroponic systems, particularly the true high weight constructions.

What you will need to construct your own one of a kind fundamental Aeroponic system:
• Container to maintain the growing system (an archive).
• Submersible fountain/lake siphon.

- Tubing to sprinkle water out of the stock manual to the sprinkler heads in the growing system.
- Enclosed growing chamber for the root zone.
- Mister/sprinkler heads.
- Watertight holder to your growing chamber in which the plants' root constructions will be.
- Tubing to reestablish the surplus enhancement plan of activity back to the shop.
- Timer (like an alarm clock) to along with the siphon.

How the aeroponic system works is really a fundamental notion. First the inspiration driving the roots hanging in midair is so they can find the best ratio of oxygen they can get. The high quantity of oxygen the roots get enables the plans to grow faster than they'd normally, and also the fundamental positive position for this type of hydroponic system.

Second, there's normally no growing media utilized, revealing each the plants' roots. The plants have been suspended by small holders, or closed cell foam plugs that go around the plants' stems. These containers or polyurethane fittings match in small openings in the most elevated intention of this growing room. The roots hang down within the growing room where they get sprinkled with nutritional supplement from mister heads in regular short cycles. The normal watering cycles keep the roots from drying out, similarly as it provides the enhancements that the plants will need to grow.

In the growing room the roots must be assured of light, and nearly fixed closed. It ought to allow fresh air in so the roots can find a whole lot of oxygen; however, you should not bother using water to evaporate, or problems can occur. Additionally, you will need the main room to maintain in wetness. In the long term what you will need is for your roots to receive a whole lot of moistness, fresh oxygen, and enrichments. An inside and outside organized aeroponics structure provides a reasonable amount of all the three of these elements to the roots at exactly the exact same time.

All in all, a principle believed in aeroponic systems would be the water dot size. Roots sprinkled with a nice haze will grow considerably quicker, bushier, and also allow the surface area to absorb oxygen and enrichments more than roots showered with little flashes of water such as from small sprinkler heads. That changes over to the plant overhang building up much more rapidly too. Aeroponic system forms are requested based on the water dab dimensions.

There are 3 kinds of Aeroponic Systems

Low Weight Aeroponic Systems (soakaponics)
In a like manner called "soakaponics" low-weight reduction structures are exactly what most by far consider when they think of aeroponics.

That's on a really basic level taking into consideration the way most aeroponic systems offered at shops selling hydroponics supplies are reduced weight constructions. While the very low weight structures operate agreeably, the water that is colossal dab size is completely different than in the large weight systems.

The guideline reason why the very low weight systems are so prominent is they don't require considerably longer in the plan for the price or exceptional assembling than many other forms of semi-automatic structures. The simplicity and minimal effort of low weight programs makes this type of aeroponic structure surprisingly good for numerous home manufacturers.

You don't have to mess with any outstanding preparation or special water siphon. The conventional fountain/lake siphons will do fine. You do in any case require a siphon that's much more grounded than you need another type of hydroponic construction. That's the key and the highest sophistication. That's in light of how the weight from the structure will fall somewhat with every sprinkler head you incorporate. Fountain and pond siphons do not offer a psi (weight) evaluation, yet the greater GPH (gallons per hour) it may put out is nearer to the "top head height" the longer grounded (fatter) the siphon is.

You will need enough sprinkler heads for the area the scatter covers, and that completely covers the whole root zone actually, as the crops become larger and the root mass gets bigger. When the root mass becomes colossal, it is regularly difficult for the shower from the sprinkler heads to invade the thick root mass. If you happen to structure your low-fat reduction system so that the roots have been showered from within the main density or near its elevated stage, the water will evaporate through the main mass a lot better than attempting to water them from beneath.

HYDROPONICS   AEROPONICS

 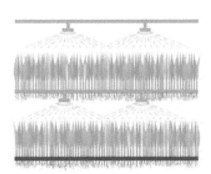

High Weight Aeroponic Systems (real aeroponic structures)

Even though the low weight structures would be the most commonly perceived, higher weight reduction systems would be the "real aeroponic" systems. That's in light of how it requires the greater weight (60-90 psi) to appropriately atomize the water into a nice haze with just a tiny water jolt in size. This fine mist enables the roots to have more oxygen than in reduced weight constructions. At any rate it is logically uncontrollable and very expensive to construct a high weight aeroponic construction.

What you will need to collect your own real high-weight Aeroponic structure:

• Accumulator tank (to act as the pressurized shop tank).
• Solenoid valve (to start and shut the feed to the mister heads).
• Alarm clock (to start and shut the solenoid valve).
• Nice shower mister heads (to sprinkle the roots with a nice haze).
• Little air blower (to pressurize the aggregator tank).
• Enclosed growing room for the root zone.
• A set supply to build the overflow if you would like to reuse the improvement plan of action.

Even though the fundamental structure of this growing plant and chamber sponsorship can move as before comparably similarly with low weight loss systems, the water (supplement plan of activity) transportation structure is completely different. In outlook on just how every now and again a siphon would have to execute and (100s to 1,000s of times daily) it'd run out fast. Hence that the water siphon is lost in large weight reduction structures.

To do that they pressurize the inventory. The very obvious way to cope with do this is by employing a gatherer tank such as the kind employed in RO (rearrange absorption) water methods. It is in an overall sense a tank using a flexible divider/stomach inside, which makes a variety of sides. Water (supplement plans) goes in 1 side, and compressed air moves in another. The air is filled until the weight comes to approximately 60 to 90 psi. That burden pushes against the flexible stomach and pressurizes the shop side with the enhancement program in it to some similar psi.

A water line continues operating in the store to the mister heads at the encased growing room to mist the roots. A Solenoid valve is used to start and shut the water traveling through the line into the mister heads. The Solenoid valve open and shut organizing is driven by means of a cycle clock. T he cycle clock may open and shut the Solenoid for as few as one minute, according to the manufacturer requirements. Consistently it is open/on for only a couple of minutes at a continuous progression, and away for just minutes until it sprinkles again. The cycle clock shuts and opens the Solenoid watering the plants roots with mist in this type of "on/off cycle" all day and night.

Ultrasonic foggers

Ultrasonic foggers have likewise been utilized to create a mist in aeroponic constructions, at any rate with mixed outcomes. Ultrasonic foggers are mostly used to create visual looks in lakes, equally as before a bunch of individuals. They're also often sold around Halloween with the Halloween decorations. While they do create a haze with just a tiny water sprinkling dimension, there's absolutely no real sogginess from the haze/murkiness.

The mist generated utilizing ultrasonic foggers in a similar manner will when all is said and done fall to the bottom of this compartment. This makes it difficult to ensure the roots are completely covered from the haze continually. Another problem with using foggers is the plates will when all is said in done interfere with nutrient construction.

The basic plates which seem to function with any lasting quality would be the expensive Teflon heads. They can part of the time be washed with white vinegar, or water and pH down, and then tidying them up using a Q-tip. A few growers have united using ultrasonic foggers near by the very low weight reduction structure in a comparative system.

Aeroponic structures would be the very "front " hydroponic plans which you are able to collect. Regardless, they are not so complicated as soon as you perceive how they operate.

A direct aeroponic structure can work in your home.

An Aeroponic system looks like an NFT structure as the roots are usually suspended in the air. What makes a difference is an aeroponic structure accomplishes this by blurring the main canal using an improvement plan of action consistently instead of conducting a small picture of supplement plan along a station.

A few cultivators will need to mist on a cycle such as a rhythmic growth structure, anyhow the cycle is a lot shorter, usually only holding up a couple of minutes between every obfuscating. It is in like fashion possible to mist a constant preface and utilize a superior sprayer to guarantee more oxygen gets into the root canal.

Aeroponic structures are seen to make plants grow a whole lot faster than a portion of the troublesome systems like heavy water culture, anyhow this hasn't yet been assessed to be valid in all scenarios. In case you need to explore many avenues concerning the structure, you may call for specific shower spouts to atomize the growing system.

Factors of interest of Aeroponics:

• Roots frequently are exposed to more oxygen than submerged-root systems

Downsides of Aeroponics:

• High-weight spouts can miss the mark and roots can dry out

• Not as discreet or simple to formulate as many other procedures

How to Build Your Own Hydroponic System

Now comes the interesting part! Growing

First you need to choose a growing medium. You will find a whole plethora of different mediums which have been utilized over time. They comprise rockwool, sawdust, peat, pearlite, vermiculite, sand, gravel, and various inert mixtures. You may probably use the majority of these mediums in this system, but allow me to boil it down to 2 options for you - pearlite and expanded clay pellets (bay pour, grow rocks, geolite).

Pearlite it great as it is dirt cheap, about 10 bucks for 4 feet. That'll fill over nine systems! As soon as your harvest is completed you can just throw it away and start with new pearlite. You do not need to think about cleaning and sterilizing your own medium.

The clay pellets work well also, they're the alternative for commercial hydroponic farmers in Holland (the territory of hydroponics and greenhouses). They last a long time and they're guaranteed not to make a difference in your nutrient balance.

The downside to using the expanded clay is that it's costly. They cost 10 bucks for 3.5 gallons - that is nine times more costly! As you'll not be throwing the clay pellets away, as I advise using them for long-term crops.

Since you have your medium in hand, with your crops and your freshly made "Aquafarm," we are all set to have fun. First off, why we did not paste the drip ring on the pump column is so we can push it away and get it out of our way once we fill out the growing room with medium and plants! Thus....push that sucker away today! Then fill out the growing room with your medium. Be certain not to fill it any more than the amount of the drip ring. You can adjust the degree of the pump column and then drip ring by shifting the pvc support tubing down and up (ahaaaa!! …. that's why it fit tightly in the pit) as essential. If you're utilizing pearlite, I suggest that they you pre-wet it using plain old water. Give it a fairly good soaking using a hose and allow the excess water to drain away (make sure you dump the extra water from this nutrient reservoir). If you're transplanting from soil, gently wash the soil from the root ball as much as you can.

It's not necessary to eliminate all the soil, just as much as you can without mauling the main system. In case you've begun your plants in rockwool cubes, vegetable sticks or peat pellets just plant the entire thing.

Then find that trickle ring and maintain in its location for a moment. Use the precise science of imagining and have a notion of where the middle of this ring is in connection to the bucket.

Set the drip ring and make a hole where you decided the center should be. Gently put your plant into the hole, evenly dispersing its roots. Backfill the hole. Locate that trickle ring. Unplug 1 end of this ring in the top. Set the ring back on the pump column, then wrap the ring round the stem of the plant, and then plug it back into the top. Last, fill the reservoir with 2.5 gallons of nutrient solution. Just gradually pour it directly into the growing system.

Connect the tank pump into the 3/16" tubing onto the pump column and then plug the pump in. The pillar must immediately begin pumping up nutrient from this reservoir and then drip it round the bottom of the plant. It's better for you to use a very simple light timer to turn the pump on during daytime hours and away throughout the night-time.

Happy Hydroponic Gardening!
A note about nutrients... I strongly suggest the usage of this General Hydroponics lineup of nutrients. GH is regarded as the very best nutrient maker by the hydroponic community.
So great that the USDA, the EPA and NASA uses them.

They make four distinct kinds of nutrient, which range from a "beginner-no-brainer" one part powder of a 3 component liquid system (can you say, "turbo charge your plants?").

The General Hydroponics Controller/reservoir system automatically keeps the correct fluid level in several units that are growing. It's compatible with all the Water Farm, Power Grower and Aquafarm modules. By feeding all of your plants from one source, you do not have to track the fluid thickness, pH and PPM of every individual module, but just of one reservoir. The massive reservoir also enables you to forget about tending your garden should you go away for a couple of days.

Assembly

Organize the growing modules in either a double or single row on a flat surface. The controller may accommodate up to 8 modules. Insert the right fitting into the grommet near the base of the controller. Add a vest fitting to the grommet near the base of every module. Put the elbow fitting in the previous module(s). Connect the modules and control container together utilizing the blue plastic tubing.

Insert the drain tube to the grommet on the other side of the control. Add the float valve to the control and join the brass barb fitting.

Insert the nutrient solution into the control container until each of the modules are satisfied with the appropriate level along with the float valve shuts off the flow. Fix the float valve pole by bending up or down to adjust the amount from the modules. Put the lid on the control and sit reservoir in addition to controller container. Add the right fitting to the grommet near the base of the reservoir and then attach the blue plastic tubing into the matching one and the control's barbed brass fitting. Fill the reservoir with the nutrient solution.

General Troubleshooting Guides and Mistakes to Avoid

If white salt residue forms on the GROROX:

1. Consider using a milder nutrient solution and topping off with plain water only.

2. Sometimes drain your system, refill with plain water and then operate the pump immediately. Following the overnight exfoliate, empty reservoir, wash and fill with new nutrient.

If plants aren't growing nicely and you guess "hard" water:

1. Try purified or distilled water. You need to see a substantial improvement in plant health and growth within a week.

2. Collect rainwater to be used in your system.

If nutrient solution stops flowing out of the drip ring:

1. Check to make sure that the pump is plugged in and reservoir is full of nutrient solution.

2. Disconnect air line from the air inlet and then assess if the air is coming through (place end under water and look for bubbles). No air leak may indicate the pump is broken and has to be replaced or the airline is either blocked or loose. Consider cutting an inch off each end of this line to provide a tighter match.

3. Blow in the air inlet to assess whether it's clogged. Scrub the pumping pillar in warm water. This sort of clogging is generally a sign you've got hard water or too powerful a nutrient solution.

4. Assess whether emitter holes at the drip ring are obstructed. To clean, disassemble drip ring by pulling it apart at the top, rinse drip band and top hot water and clean the holes using a toothpick.

How frequently should the reservoir be emptied along with the nutrient solution changed?
The reservoir ought to be emptied and washed every 7-10 days.

Definitely drain and wash whenever you alter the nutrient ratio formulation. Additionally, it's a great idea to wash off the rising media whenever the reservoir is washed. Plant waste will have a tendency to collect on the rising media.

When reservoir levels start to shed, should it be topped off with fresh water or nutrient solution?

Normally nutrient strength should operate between 800 to 1,200 parts per million (PPM). To quantify PPM, you'll need to buy a nutrient testing apparatus and begin tracking your nutrient solution. We use meters using a "sodium chloride" scale.

When in doubt, recall that it's almost always better to apply a little nutrient than a lot of, and if you don't understand the particular PPM tolerance level for the plant you're growing, it's ideal to maintain the nutrient solution between 800 and 1,200 PPM.

Assembly Guide FARM

Setup
The growing chamber, stuffed with Grorox, sits at the reservoir container.

The pumping column fits into the pumping tube, reaching to the nutrient solution found in the reservoir. Air pressure in the pump pushes up the solution through the pumping pillar into the drip ring, and that is joined to the column using a tee connector, with the drip holes facing down. Solution drains into the drain/level tube elbow, which can be inserted through the rubber grommet in the base of the reservoir.

Step #1.

Add black clip.

Step # 2.

Install the blue drain/level tube across the exterior of this reservoir. Moisten the end of the elbow fitting and shove through the rubber grommet in the surface till the next ridge passes the grommet. As you push, then put your other hand within the reservoir over the grommet to encourage it, or so the grommet doesn't pop out.

The tube fits to the clip on top of the reservoir. If the grommet pops out, then push it back in (the broader ending points). If water flows from this region following the reservoir is full be certain that the blue tube fits snugly onto the elbow.

Fill the reservoir into the white line indicated on the gloomy drain/level tube, with tap water.

Insert General Hydroponics nutrient according to instructions on the label.

Step #3.

Set the growing chamber onto the reservoir.

Step #4.

Push the column support tube (the white PVC pipe), with the beveled end, into the huge hole found in the base of the growing chamber so that it protrudes down to the reservoir. Fix it so its top arrives to an inch below the rim of the growing chamber.

Step #5.

Attach the round drip ring into the T fitting. Make certain holes in the drip ring are facing down.

Step # 6.

Push the whole drip ring assembly (which contains the drip ring, then the T fitting along with the white tubes connected to the drip ring) into the pumping tube. It's a great idea to disassemble and wash the drip ring collecting and draining pipe from time to time in warm water.

Step # 7.

Move drip ring out of the way and put the bag of Grorox into the growing chamber.

Step # 8.

Securely attach the air tubing (the thin, elastic, clear tubing on the drip ring assembly) into the socket nipple on the pump. Plug into any standard household electrical outlet. If you are using your farm outdoors, use only extension cords and sockets made for outside usage.

Planting

To prepare a seedling or a plant for transplanting, eliminate all organic or soil substance from around the roots. Plants have to be hardy with established roots prior to transplantation to the farm. Choose seedlings, since it is more challenging to successfully transplant elderly plants.

If your plant was growing in soil or peat moss, then lightly remove the plant from the pot and carefully wash as much soil as you can from the roots prior to repainting.

Though this way of transplanting from soil into hydroponics is somewhat insecure, (soil could contain diseased organisms which proliferate from the rich hydroponic solution), we've been quite effective in executing it, especially with culinary herbs and also invite you to attempt it.

Or, you can prevent these issues by starting plants from cuttings in among our Rain Forest hydroponic systems.

If you intend to grow several tiny plants in the farm, put your plants just beyond the drip ring, close to the drip holes. If you would rather have a single large plant, then put it at the middle of the drip ring. Gradually add Grorox around the plant roots until completely coated.

Power Grower Setup Instructions.

Setup

The growing chamber, stuffed with Grorox, sits at the reservoir container. The pumping column fits into the pumping tube, reaching to the nutrient solution found in the reservoir. Air pressure in the pump pushes up the solution through the pumping pillar into the drip ring, and that is joined to the column using a tee, and making drip holes. Solution drains into the drain/level tube elbow, which can be inserted through the rubber grommet in the base of the reservoir.

Assembly Instructions

Step #1.

Securely connect the air tube (the thin, elastic, clear tubing on the drip ring gathering) into the socket nipple on the pump.

Step #2.

Fill the reservoir at precisely an inch above the white line indicated on the blue double function tubing, with tap water. Insert General Hydroponics nutrient according to instructions on the label.

Step #3.

Directions for the discretionary Power Grower Base. Put the reservoir onto the bottom, make sure the electrical cable and air tube each emerge individually from the air pump through notches located in the base.

Step #4.

Insert each of the legs (the extended plastic pipes with slits) to each of the four indentations from the perforated bottom of the growing chamber.

Push the slotted ends to the openings so that they fit snugly. These legs encourage the growing room when removing for cleaning.

Step #5.

Set the growing chamber in the reservoir. Push the pumping pipe (the residual plastic pipe) into the massive hole found in the base of the growing room so that it flows down to the reservoir. Fix it so that its top comes to an inch below the rim of the growing chamber.

Step #6.

Eliminate sand and other debris, then pour Grorox into reservoir and then wash. Soak Grorox immediately in nutrient solution into precondition, then empty Grorox from reservoir in the Growing Chamber into a degree of 3 inches.

Step #7.

If your plant has been growing in soil or peat moss, lightly remove the plant from its pot and carefully wipe as much soil as you can from the roots prior to transplanting.

Though this way of transplanting from soil into hydroponics is somewhat insecure, (soil could contain diseased organisms which proliferate from the wealthy hydroponic solution), we've been quite effective in executing it, especially with culinary herbs and also invite you to attempt.

Or, you can prevent these issues by starting plants from cuttings in among our Rain Forest hydroponic systems.

Step #7a.

If you plan to grow several tiny plants at the Power Grower, put your plants just beyond the drip ring, close to the drip holes. If you would rather have a single large plant, then put it at the middle of the drip ring. Gradually add Grorox around the plant roots before thoroughly coated.

Step #8.

Attach the circular brown drip ring into the T-clamp by shoving each end of the drip ring. Push the whole drip ring assembly (which contains the drip ring, then the T-clamp along with the white tubes connected to the drip ring clamp) down to the pumping tube so the entire assembly rests, or slightly over, the Grorox. It's a great idea to disassemble and wash the drip ring gathering and draining pipe from time to time in warm water.

Step #9.

Attach the air tube that's on the air pump to the rigid narrow tube of this drip ring gathering emerging out of the pumping tube.

Step #10.

Plug your Power Grower into any standard household electrical outlet. If you are using your Power outside, use only extension cords and sockets made for outside usage.

Abundant light, appropriate temperature and sufficient ventilation are critical for rapid growth, healthy crops and high yields. Put the Power Grower in a hot, well-lit, well-ventilated place, like an outdoor garden, sunlit window, patio or greenhouse. And needless to say, keep your Power Grower away from regions where the inevitable leaking that happens during draining, filling and pH adjustment can lead to water damage

Operation

For moisture-loving plants, operate your Power Grower pump consistently. Plants preferring drier conditions grow best when the pump works for 12 hours and can be off for 12 hours (a very simple timer will turn the pump off and on for you automatically).

Use medium to regular strength nutrient solution and avoid powerful or competitive nutrient. As your crops absorb nutrient solution, the amount in the reservoir will fall. Top off with half power solution or plain water (the pump is much more effective once the reservoir is complete). It's vital to alter the nutrients and water every two to three months, just drain the reservoir by rotating the murky double function tubing 90 degrees so water drains onto the floor, or inside a pail. When altering or topping off option, pour straight over the Grorox (instead of to the reservoir) to flush out excess salts.

Planning for Replanting

After harvesting and before replanting your Power Grower, dismantle the machine and wash all parts with warm water. Rinse Grorox in hot water and soak overnight. Contrary to Rockwool, Grorox is also reusable.

Eve's Garden Setup Directions

Congratulations on your choice of the Eve's Garden (Dutch Garden), the state of the art system in contemporary hydroponics. The Eve's Garden may be utilized in a greenhouse, on a deck or patio and inside under lights. We anticipate a growing achievement and welcome the chance to serve you through the next several years.

Step #1.

Attach both the sawhorse brackets and legs on the cross braces.

Step #2.

Screw pump line onto pump. Place pump to reservoir by adding the conclusion of pump line via the hole in the lid of the reservoir. Put pump parallel into left side of reservoir, putting power cable through cutout in lid. Lift drain end of construction and slip the reservoir below the drain tube; align tube with big hole. Put black drip line, with connected spaghetti tube, along with drain railing. With elbow fitting extending beyond drain railing, screw elbow on pump line. Attach the lattice into the bottom of the service rail with screws.

Step #3.

Insert drain fittings into every Dutch pot. The smaller end of drain matching fits into pit on top ledge; broad end fits over plastic expansion situated in bottom of the pot.

Step #4.

Open the bag of Grorox and wash thoroughly with plain water.

Fill up the Dutch pots up to an inch over the drain fittings. Reserve a similar quantity of Grorox for high mulch (Step 5).

The remaining Grorox is going to be combined with ready cocopeat (Step 5). Notice: 1 13.2 gallon tote of Grorox, when blended with all the 3 cocopeat bricks, may fill both Dutch pots.

Step #5.

Fill a 5 gallon bucket with 3 liters of water and set the 3 bricks of Cocopeat into the bucket of water. Soak before the Cocopeat bricks into a soil like material. Thoroughly combine the Grorox with the Cocopeat and fill up the Dutch Pots for this mix. Best dress the Dutch Pots with 1" of Grorox.

Step #6.

Prepare your seedling or plant for transplanting by removing and draining all organic or soil substance from around the roots. It's ideal to decide on seedlings as it's more challenging to transplant plants. Then set the seedling or plant into the Grorox/Cocopeat mix. It's possible, naturally, to start with seeds by planting them just as you would with soil.

Step #7.

Position the Dutch Pots on the support railing and into one of those holes around the drain railing.

Then attach the drip bits to the end of their spaghetti tubes. Insert the pointed end of the trickle stakes into the Dutch Pots close to the crops. Insert any unused spaghetti lines into the tiny brownish cap plugs. Add the cap plugs to the unused holes onto the drain railing.

Planning and Building a Greenhouse.

Careful planning is significant prior to starting a house greenhouse job. Building a greenhouse doesn't have to be costly or time-consuming. The final selection of the kind of greenhouse will be contingent on the growing space needed, home design, accessible websites, and prices. The greenhouse has to, nevertheless, provide suitable air for growing plants.

Location

The greenhouse should be located where it gets maximum sun. The primary choice of a place is the south or southeast side of a structure or shade trees. Sunlight all day is best, but morning sun on the east side is adequate for crops. Morning sunlight is the most desirable since it permits the plant's food manufacturing process to start early; hence growth is maximized. An east side place captures the maximum November to February sun. The subsequent best sites are west and south of important structures, where crops get sun later in the day. North of important constructions is the least desired place and is great just for plants that need a little mild sun.

Deciduous trees, such as maple and walnut, can effectively shade the greenhouse in the extreme late afternoon summer sun nonetheless, they shouldn't shade the greenhouse in the daytime. Deciduous trees also allow maximum exposure to sunlight since they drop their leaves in the autumn. Evergreen trees which have foliage all year long shouldn't be found where they will shade the greenhouse since they'll block the intense winter sunshine. You need to aim to optimize sunlight exposure, especially if the rainwater is used annually. Bear in mind that the sun is lower in the southern skies in winter causing long shadows to be cast by buildings and trees that are evergreen.

Great drainage is a different requirement for the site. If required, assemble the greenhouse over the surrounding floor so rain and irrigation water will drain off. Other site factors include the light needs of these plants needing to be increased; places of sources of water, heat, and power; and shelter in cold weather. Access to the greenhouse ought to be suitable for both utilities and people. An office for potting plants and also a storage space for supplies needs to be nearby.

Types of Greenhouses

A home greenhouse can be set in a home or garage, or it may be a freestanding structure. The preferred site and personal taste can dictate the options to be considered. An attached greenhouse could be a half greenhouse, a full size construction, or an elongated window structure. There are benefits and disadvantages to each type.

Attached Greenhouses

Lean-to. A lean-to rainwater is a half greenhouse, divided across the summit of the roof, or ridge line, lean-tos are used where space is restricted to a diameter of about seven to twelve feet, and they're the cheapest constructions. The ridge of this lean-to is connected to your construction using a single side and a present door, if accessible.

Lean-tos are near accessible power, water and warmth. The downsides include some constraints on space, ventilation, sunlight, and temperature management. The height of the supporting wall restricts the possible size of this lean-to. The wider the lean-to, the greater the supporting wall has to be. Temperature control is harder since the walls which the greenhouse is constructed on will collect the sun's warmth while the translucent cover of this greenhouse may eliminate heat quickly.

The lean-to should tackle the ideal method for adequate sunlight exposure. Last, think about the positioning of doors and windows on the supporting construction and keep in mind that snow, ice, or rain may slide off the roof or your home onto the building.

Even-span. An even-span is a full-size structure which includes one gable end connected to a different building. It's generally the biggest and most expensive alternative, but it provides more usable space and may be lengthened. The even-span has a much better shape compared to the usual lean-to for air flow to keep uniform temperatures throughout the winter heating season. An even-span can accommodate two to three spaces for growing crops.

Window-mounted. A window-mounted greenhouse could be mounted to the south or south side of a home. This glass enclosure provides room for handily growing several plants at comparatively low prices. The exceptional window extends outward in the house a foot or so and may comprise a couple of shelves.

Freestanding Structures

Freestanding greenhouses are different structures; they are sometimes set apart from other buildings for sunlight and can be made as big or small as needed. Another heating process is necessary, and water and electricity have to be set up.

The lowest price per square foot of growing space is usually offered in a freestanding or even-span greenhouse that's 17 to 18 feet wide. It may house a central area, two side chairs, and two paths. The proportion of price into the usable growing space is great. When choosing the kind of building, make sure you plan for sufficient area space, storage area, and space for future growth.

Massive greenhouses are simpler to handle because temperatures in tiny greenhouses differ more quickly.

Little greenhouses have a large exposed area by which heat is gained or lost, along with the air volume inside is comparatively modest; hence, the air temperature changes rapidly in a little greenhouse. Suggested minimum dimensions are 6 ft wide by 12 ft extended to get an even-span or freestanding greenhouse.

Structural Materials

A fantastic selection of industrial greenhouse frames and framing stuff can be found. The frames are made from wood, stainless steel, or aluminum. Build-it-yourself greenhouse programs are often for structures with metal or wood pipe frames. Vinyl pipe substances generally are insufficient to fulfill snow and wind load requirements. Frames can be coated with glass, stiff fiberglass, stiff double-wall plastics, or plastic film. All have benefits and disadvantages. Every one of those materials must be considered--it pays to shop around to get ideas.

Frames

Greenhouse frames range from simple to complicated, based upon the creativity of the designer and technology demands. Listed below are some common frames.

Quonset.

The Quonset is really a straightforward and efficient structure with an electric conduit or stainless steel pipe framework. The framework is circular and generally covered with plastic sheeting. Quonset sidewall height is reduced, which limits storage space and head room.

Gothic.

The gothic frame structure is comparable to that of the Quonset however, it's a gothic form. Wooden arches might be utilized and combined at the form. The gothic form allows more head room in the sidewall compared to the Quonset.

Rigid-frame. The Rigid-frame construction has vertical sidewalls and rafters to get a clear-span structure. There are no trusses or columns to support the roofing. Glued or plywood gussets connect the sidewall supports into the rafters to create one stiff framework. The traditional gable roof and sidewalls enable maximum interior space and air flow. A fantastic base is needed to support the lateral load onto the sidewalls.

Post and rafter and A-frame. The post and rafter are an easy structure of an embedded post and rafters, but it needs more metal or wood than some other layouts.

Powerful sidewall articles and heavy post embedment are needed to withstand external rafter forces and end pressures. Such as the stiff framework, the pole and rafter design enable more distance across the sidewalls and efficient air flow. The A-frame is much like the post and rafter structure except a collar beam links the top elements of the rafters together.

Coverings

Greenhouse coverings include long-life ceramic, glass, stiff double-wall plastics, and film plastics with 1- to 3-year lifespans. The kind of framework and cover has to be fitted properly.

Glass

Glass is the traditional covering. It has a pleasing look, is cheap to maintain, and contains a high level of permanency. An aluminum frame with a glass covering supplies a maintenance-free, weather-tight construction which reduces heat expenses and keeps in humidity. Glass can be found in a number of types that would be appropriate with just about any style or design. Tempered glass is often used because it's two or three times more powerful than normal glass.

Small prefabricated glass greenhouses are offered for do it-yourself setup, but should be constructed from the manufacturer since they are sometimes hard to build. The downsides of glass will be that it's readily broken, is really expensive to construct, and needs much better framework structure than plastic or fiberglass. A fantastic base is needed, along with the frames have to be powerful and has to fit well with each other to support thick, inflexible glass.

Fiberglass

Fiberglass is lightweight, powerful, and nearly hail proof. A fantastic grade of fiberglass must be utilized because inferior grades discolor and decrease light penetration. Use only clear, transparent, or translucent levels for greenhouse building. Tedlar-coated fiberglass lasts 15 to 20 decades. The resin covering the bark fibers will gradually wear off, allowing soil to be kept by fibers that are exposed. A fresh coat of resin is necessary following 10 to 15 decades. Light penetration is as great as glass, but can shed substantially over time with inferior levels of fiberglass.

Double-wall plastic. Rigid double-layer vinyl sheets of acrylic or polycarbonate can be found to offer long-life, heat-saving covers. These covers include two layers of plastic split by webs.

The double layer substance retains more heat, therefore energy savings of 30% are typical. The oil is a long-life, nonyellowing substance; the polycarbonate normally yellows quicker, but generally is shielded by a UV inhibitor coating onto the exposed surface.

Both substances carry guarantees for 10 years in their light transmission qualities. Both may be used on curved surfaces; the polycarbonate material could be curved more. As a rule of thumb, each coating reduces light by roughly 10 percent. Approximately 80% of the light filters via double-layer vinyl, compared with 90% for glass.

Film-plastic

Film-plastic coverings can be found in a number of ranges of quality and many unique materials. Ordinarily, these are replaced more often than other covers. Structural costs are extremely low because the framework can be plastic and lighter film is affordable. Light transmission of those film-plastic coverings is similar to glass. The movies are produced from polyethylene (PE), polyvinyl chloride (PVC), copolymers, and other substances.

A utility grade of PE that will last about a year can be found in local hardware stores.

Industrial greenhouse grade PE contains ultraviolet inhibitors on it to shield against ultraviolet rays; it lasts 12 to 18 months. Copolymers last 2-3 decades. New additives have let the manufacture of picture plastics which obstruct and reflect radiated heat back in the greenhouse, as does glass that will help reduce heating expenses. PVC or vinyl movie costs two to five times as far as PE, however lasts as long as five decades. But, it's available only in sheets four to six feet wide. It attracts dust out of the air; therefore, it has to be cleaned sometimes.

Foundations and Floors

Permanent foundations should be supplied for ceramic, glass, or even the double-layer rigid-plastic sheet stuff. The manufacturer should supply plans for the base structure. Most home greenhouses need a poured concrete base like people in residential homes. Quonset greenhouses with pipe frames along with a plastic cover utilize articles driven into the floor.

Engineered floors aren't recommended since it might remain moist and slippery from soil mix media. A concrete, gravel, or rock walkway 24 to 36 inches wide may be constructed for simple access to plants. The remaining part of the floor ought to be covered by several inches of gravel for drainage of excess water. Water can also be sprayed on the soil to generate moisture in the greenhouse.

Environmental Systems

Greenhouses provide a refuge where a suitable environment is preserved for plants. Solar energy from sunlight offers sunlight and some warmth, but you have to offer a method to control the environment from your greenhouse. This is carried out by using heaters, fans, thermostats, and other gear.

Heating

The heating prerequisites of a greenhouse are determined by the desirable temperature for the crops grown, the place and construction of the greenhouse, as well as the complete outside exposed region of the building. Just as 25% of the daily heat condition may come in sunlight, however a lightly insulated greenhouse construction will require a lot of warmth on a cold winter night. The heating system has to be sufficient to keep the day or nighttime temperature.

Normally the house heating system isn't sufficient to heat an adjoining greenhouse. A 220-volt circuit electrical heater, however, is tidy, efficient, and functions nicely. Little oil or gas heaters made to be set up via a masonry wall also do the job nicely. Solar-heated greenhouses were widely popular temporarily during the energy crisis, but they didn't prove to be more economical to use.

Independent solar and storage collection systems are big and need much space. But greenhouse owners may experiment with heat-collecting procedures to lessen fossil-fuel intake. One technique is to paint containers to pull in warmth, and match them with water to keep it. But since the greenhouse air temperature has to be held to plant-growing temperatures, so the greenhouse itself isn't a fantastic solar-heat collector.

Heating systems may be fueled by gas, electricity, oil, or wood. The heat could be dispersed by forced hot air, radiant heating, hot water, or steam. The option of a heating fuel and system is dependent on what's locally available, the creation demands of the crops, price, and individual option. For security purposes, and also to prevent harmful gases from plants that are calling, all gasoline, petroleum, and woodburning systems should be properly vented to the exterior.

Use fresh-air vents to provide oxygen for burners for total combustion. Security controls, such as security pilots along with a gas shutoff change, should be utilized as required. Portable kerosene heaters used in homes are insecure because some plants are sensitive to fumes formed when the gas is burnt.

Air Circulation

Installing circulating lovers on your own greenhouse is a fantastic investment. During the winter once the greenhouse is heated, then you have to keep air flow so that temperatures remain uniform across the greenhouse. With no air-mixing lovers, the hot air rises to the top and cool air circulates round the plants around the ground. Small fans using a cubic-foot-per-minute (ft3/min) air-moving capacity equivalent to a quarter of their air volume of the greenhouse are adequate.

For smaller greenhouses (less than 60 ft long), set the buffs in diagonally opposite corners out in the sides and ends. The target is to create a round (oval) regular of air motion. Run the fans continuously through the winter. Turn these fans off in summer once the greenhouse will have to be ventilated.

The fan in a forced-air heating system can occasionally be utilized to present constant air flow. The fan has to be wired into a shut-off switch so it can operate continuously, different from the thermostatically controlled burner.

Ventilation

Ventilation is the exchange of inside air for external air to control temperature, eliminate moisture, or replenish carbon dioxide (CO_2). Several ventilation systems may be utilized.

Be cautious when mixing elements of 2 systems. Natural ventilation utilizes roof vents onto the ridge line with side inlet vents (louvers). Warm air rises on convective currents to escape through the surface, drawing cool air in through the sides.

Mechanical ventilation utilizes an exhaust fan to move out air from one end of the greenhouse while external air enters the opposite end through aerodynamic inlet louvers. Exhaust fans must be sized to swap the entire quantity of air in the greenhouse every moment. The entire quantity of air in a medium to large greenhouse could be estimated by multiplying the floor area instances 8.0 (the normal height of a greenhouse). A small greenhouse (less than 5,000 ft in air volume) must have an exhaust-fan capability estimated by multiplying the floor area by 12.

The capacity of this exhaust fan ought to be chosen at one-eighth of an inch static water pressure. The static stress evaluation accounts for air immunity through the louvers, lovers, and rainwater and is typically shown in the enthusiast selection graph. Ventilation requirements change with the weather and year.
An individual has to determine just how much the rainwater will be utilized. In the summer, 1 to 2 1/2 air volume varies per minute are required.

Little greenhouses require the bigger sum. In the winter, 20 to 30 percent of a single air volume market per second is adequate for mixing cool air without upsetting the crops.

One single-speed enthusiast cannot fulfill this criteria. Two single-speed fans are better. A combo of a single-speed enthusiast and a two-speed fan allows three ventilation rates which most meets year-round demands. A single-stage and also a two-stage thermostat are required to restrain the operation. A two-speed engine on a low rate produces about 70% of its entire capacity. If the 2 fans have exactly the exact same ability evaluation, then the low-speed enthusiast provides about 35% of the combined total.

This rate of venting is reasonable for winter. In spring, the fan works on top speed. In summer, the two fans operate on top speed. Consult with the earlier instance of a little greenhouse. A 16-foot broad by 24-foot long home would require an estimated ft. per second (cubic feet per second; CFM) absolute capacity; this will be, 16x24x12 ft3 per second. To be used all year, pick two fans to provide 2,300 ft. per second each, 1 fan to have two rates so the high speed is 2,300 ft. per second.
Adding the next fan, the next venting rate is the amount of both fans on high speed, or 4,600 ft. per second.

Many glass greenhouses are offered using a manual ridge port, even if a mechanical system is defined. The guide system may be a backup system; however, it doesn't take the location of a motorized louver. Don't take shortcuts in growing an automated management system.

Cooling

Air motion by ventilation alone might not be sufficient in the middle of the summer time; the air temperature might have to be reduced with underfloor heating. Additionally, the light intensity might be too good for plants. Throughout the summertime, evaporative cooling, shaded fabric, or paint may be critical. Color materials incorporate roll-up displays of aluminum or wood, vinyl sheeting, and paint. Small bundle evaporative coolers have a buff and evaporative pad at 1 box to evaporate water, which cools air and raises humidity.

Heat is removed from the air to modify water from liquid into a vapor. Moist, cooler air enters the greenhouse while heated air moves through roof vents or exhaust louvers. The evaporative cooler works great when the humidity of the outside air is reduced. The machine may be utilized without water flow to present the venting of this greenhouse.

Size the evaporative cooler capability in 1.0 to 1.5 times the size of the greenhouse. An alternate system, used in commercial greenhouses, puts the pads onto the air inlets at the same end of the greenhouse and also utilizes the exhaust fans in the opposite end of the greenhouse to pull the air throughout the home.

Controllers/Automation

An automated controller is essential to keep a sensible environment in the greenhouse. On a chilly day with varying levels of sun and clouds, the temperature may differ considerably; close oversight could be needed if a manual venting system had been in use. As a result, unless close observation is possible, both amateurs and industrial operators must have automatic methods with thermostats or additional detectors.

Thermostats may be used to control individual units, or even a central control with a single temperature sensor may be utilized. In any scenario, the sensor or sensors should be protected from sunlight, located around plant elevation from the sidewalls, also have continuous airflow.

An aspirated box is indicated; the box homes each detector and contains a little fan that puts the greenhouse air through the box and above the detector.

The box ought to be painted white so that it will reflect solar heating and permit precise readings of the air temperature.

Watering Systems

A water source is essential. Hand watering is suitable for many greenhouse plants if a person is available once the job has to be performed; but several amateurs work from home throughout the day. A number of automatic watering systems can be found to help to perform the job over brief intervals. Remember, the little greenhouse is very likely to have an assortment of plant containers, materials, and soil combinations that require various quantities of water. Time clocks or mechanical wattage detectors may be utilized to control automated watering systems. Mist sprays may be used to make humidity or to moisten seedlings. Watering kits are available to water plants in flats, benches, or baskets.

CO2 and Light

Carbon dioxide (CO_2) and light are crucial for plant growth. Since the sun climbs in the daytime to present light, the plants start to produce food energy (photosynthesis). The degree of CO_2 drops from the greenhouse since it's utilized by plants.

Ventilation replenishes the CO_2 from the greenhouse. Since CO_2 and light match each other, electrical lighting with CO_2 injection are utilized to raise yields of flowering and vegetable plants. Bottled CO_2, dry ice, and combustion of sulfur-free fuels may be utilized as CO_2 sources. Commercial greenhouses utilize such procedures.

Option Growing Structures

A greenhouse isn't always required for growing plants. Plants could be germinated in one's house in a warm area under fluorescent lamps. The lamps need to be close together rather than hanging over the plants. A cold period or hotbed may be used outdoors to last the rise of young seedlings until the weather permits planting in a garden. A hotbed is like the cold period, but it's a supply of heat to keep proper temperatures.

Choosing the Right Hydroponic System

Picking the right system is a significant choice. There are quite a few queries to be considered: How big an area does you need to cultivate? Would you only need one module, or whole system? You may expect to attain extraordinary results, but you have got to pick the ideal system. You might intend to push the system to the maximum by spending substantial time beginning crops, pruning and nurturing; or only need a low maintenance module to power-drive one or a couple of plants via an outstanding growth cycle. Nonetheless, only spending a couple of minutes every couple of days adapting to the machine.

All these are distinct demands, and we've got the systems which will meet these requirements. Single module farmers or small setup growers who desire top results without a lot of effort need to have a look at the Water Farm and Power Grower. Every one of these systems may be operated as only standalone modules, or interconnected in-groups of 2 to three modules with the optional control systems. For propagating cuttings or quick-starting seeds, transplants or seedlings, there's not any hydroponic system which will match the performance of the Rain Forest.

The AeroFlo requires regular attention because growth rates are extremely significant. Abundant and good quality clean water and power has to be easily available. The effective grower will track the machine and plants, constantly ensuring their requirements are fulfilled. Rapidly growing plants have to be kept. Vines need trellising (external reinforcement). Fruit and flowers have to be chosen in a timely way. New plants have to be launched as mature plants complete their life cycles.

Running an AeroFlo is similar to driving an extremely fast car, the grower should look ahead and anticipate what is to come. Larger growers who need a bigger system need to take a look at the Eve's Garden (Dutch Garden). Eve's Garden includes 6 or 12 separate baskets that fit together onto a sturdy PVC framework. Eve's Garden also includes a recirculating pump, growing media, our famous Flora Nutrients and all of the hardware you need to start-you simply add the crops.

Hydroponics is somewhat like growing plants organically; it's satisfying and enjoyable. It brings us nearer to the ground, provides us with increased nutrition through improved quality meals, also helps us build a spiritual relationship with the expanding world round us.

As a way to increase our nourishment, as a teaching tool or a means to bring the household together with a common aim, there are a few more rewarding experiences than nurturing crops; humanity's oldest vocation.

Experienced hydroponic growers understand what it's like to take part in the life cycle of crops, words can't convey the feelings that a successful grower encounters watching a harvest fulfill its promise - it is a particular sort of joy; also you can experience it with one Water Farm or an enormous business setup. The hydroponic encounter will bring a new meaning into your life, one which is enjoyable, enlightening and incredibly gratifying.

Eve's Garden

We are extremely proud to offer Eve's Garden (Dutch Garden) to North American growers. This is the sole hydroponic system we provide that we didn't make here at General Hydroponics, as it was created in Holland. We've enhanced the layout for Eve's Garden we provide our distinctive beige design that's better for outside installations because the light beige colour averts solar heating.

- Imagine fresh, fragrant flowers, refreshing greens, herbs or berries right off the vine and into your salad in minutes; all growing in one Eve's Garden!
- Enjoy the capability of hydroponics in a compact, attractive package. Contains all you need (except seeds or plants) to begin!
- Assembled and ready to use in approximately twenty minutes.
- Affordable, simple and enjoyable!
- 1 Available in 6 and 12 bud variants; comes complete with reservoir, service rack, pump, GroRox, coconut fiber testing network plus a single pint of FloraGro, FloraBloom and FlorMicro nourishment.

Eve's Garden is comparable to the Aqua Farm from the plant's point of view. A container full of GroRox, or even a combo of GroRox and coconut fiber is irrigated intermittently with nutrient enriched water. A pump provides nutrient outbound in the reservoir, and spaghetti tubes provide each Dutch Pot.

Eve's Garden system is easy to operate, dependable, economical and incredibly functional. An extra benefit is that Dutch Pots full of GroRox and coconut fiber would be the first truly "organic-hydroponic" systems yet grown. This combination and our "Flora" - Advanced Nutrient System provide the very best of both worlds; organic rooting media with ultrahigh pure mineral nutrients.

Green Air Products

Dehumistat

Our DEHUMISTAT is really a popular control for eliminating unneeded atmospheric moisture collecting in an enclosed area. High humidity conditions will trigger fans or alternative dehumidifying devices until the level drops roughly 9 percent in relative humidity. At this time the gear is disabled until humidity increases again 9 percent. Switches are 110V in 10 amp maximum. Install the Dehumistat to trigger an exhaust fan or alternative dehumidifying equipment to get rid of excess humidity. The Dehumistat can be plugged right into a standard 110 VAC wall socket or to other Green Air Products timers or controls. Once plugged into the walls, like in the case above, the Dehumistat will function independently to keep humidity within your desired range.

Humistat

Control humidity automatically and correctly with Green Air Products HUMISTAT. This controller functions independently or other humidifying equipment by tripping motors, switches, pumps or valves. The 110V socket receptacle receives electricity if atmospheric moisture content gets less than your preset minimum allowable percent.

Sensor permits a 9% relaxation zone between "on" and "off" functions. Power tackling 10 amp maximum. If your furnace currently has a humidity controller, turn it to complete in place and place the humistat dial to your minimal desired humidity. The Humistat may also be employed with any humidity apparatus or some other environmentally triggered appliance. The HUMISTAT humidity switch controls humidifying equipment by providing electricity when humidity drops under the adjustable set point. Humidifiers can be exactly controlled in accordance with atmospheric humidity to produce perfect conditions for almost any surroundings.

MCC-1 Micro Climate Controller

The Micro Climate Controller MCC-1 is intended to perform all of the significant atmospheric and timed functions required in an automated growth environment such as temperature, humidity and carbon dioxide enrichment, irrigation and lighting management. The control comprises an outside coil cooling system, a dehumidifying humidistat, a 24- hour clock timer, a photo-sensor plus a repeat cycle timer. Heating and humidifying management is supplied by way of distant high-amperage relays which empower synchronized equipment administration.

Automated override and master systems organize controls to look at all probable factors. The MCC-1 is included in a black anodized, brush finish aluminum casing. An appealing screen-printed front desk with function indicator lights makes system monitoring and adjustment quick and simple. All links are standard 3-prong grounded plugs and receptacles. No hard wiring is necessary for fundamental operations. Low and higher voltage relays can be found to operate additional equipment.

Every facet of this growing environment can be addressed from the Micro Climate Controller (MCC-1). Operates on 110VAC with 15 Amp switching capability. Model 24-CT-1 Independent Outlets for Your principles in garden room restrain the 24-CT-1 may be exactly what you need. This useful thing comprises two of the common requirements of a tiny enclosure - a timed outlet along with a thermostatically controlled socket. This unit is excellent for working lights, CO_2 equipment, watering methods, fans, etc. and offers an economical option for all greenhouse management requirements.

Model CT-DH-1 Integrated Outlets

This CT-DH-1 is made to turn "On" and "Off" exhaust fans and/or intake fans to eliminate undesirable air due to heat or humidity. This unit is designed as a cooling and dehumidifying controller.

This control is great for situations where excessive heat and humidity should be removed. Internal sensors will allow a 7° temperature comfort zone and a 7% humidity interval (differential) between the time the fans go "Off" and return "On" again. Temperature rise will trigger the proper sockets and deactivate the abandoned outlets.

Model CT-DH-2 Independent Outlets

The CT-DH-2 control is intended to provide you separate outlets for heating and cooling equipment. Place the humidity and temperature dials at the desired settings. If the temperature rises beyond the set limits, the abandoned socket comes "On" and when the humidity rises, the right socket comes "On." When temperatures or humidity drop below the set limits, outlets turn "off" independently. This permits you to use a dehumidifier to control humidity and an exhaust fan to control temperature and neither side may overcome the other once they initialize. Internal detector will enable a 7° or 7 percent humidity switch between the time the gear comes "On" and extends back "off" again. Small amber lights indicate when the socket has power. Operates on 120VAC 15 Amps max. Doesn't exceed the power handling capacity of your wall socket.

Model CT-DH-3 Synchronized

Outlets- While the CT-DH-3 has many programs, it was primarily developed for use with CO_2 equipment and exhaust type fans. Internal sensors will allow a 7° temperature comfort zone and a 7% humidity (differential) between the time the fans go "off" and return "On" again. Temperature or humidity increases will activate the right-hand outlets and deactivate the left-hand sockets.

The CT-H-3 comes with an internal relay which automatically switches power from the gear side to the exhaust side of the unit when either temperature or humidity is in excess of the dial settings. Plug the controller into a 110V wall socket. Place the humidity and temperature at the desired settings. The left or right hand gear side of the control is normally at the "On" position and can trigger CO_2 gear if necessary.

Gear to be utilized for CO_2 generation ought to be plugged to the left-hand socket. All equipment required to exhaust the expanding area ought to be plugged to the right-hand socket that's the exhaust side of this control.

The left-hand socket (CO_2) is routed if the exhaust outlet is triggered. Watch optional thermostat sensors.

Also available with built-in photo sensor to conquer equipment (left) socket during darkness periods. Indicate this choice using a "P." (CT-DH-3P) Operates on 120VAC with a 12 amp switching capability.

Model CT-HT-1 Independent Outlets

This control features fully separate detectors for heating and cooling equipment. The heating thermostat causes the left-hand socket of the control, along with also the heating thermostat triggers the right-hand socket. If you need a tighter control of your temperature compared to the inner heating \ cooling thermostats, alternative sensors are available with a 4° differential.

Operates on 110VAC with 15 Amp switching capability. Twist control power cable into 110V outlet. Plug cooling gear into left-hand side sockets. Plug heating gear into appropriate side sockets. Standard thermostats are true to ± 7°. In case your growing situation demands the warmth to be no cooler than 50° without being denser than 70°, you'd place your heating system thermostat to 57° along with the heating for 63° to permit your thermostat differential. This would provide you a minimum buffer zone of 6° plus a max of 20°. Doesn't exceed the power handling capacity of your wall socket.

Tempstat

The TEMP-C temperature switch controls cooling gear by providing electricity when temperature exceeds the adjustable set point. Exhaust fans, evaporative coolers, air conditioners or ventilators could be precisely controlled in accordance with atmospheric temperature to make perfect conditions for almost any surroundings. Topical coil hydraulic sensor offers accurate reliable switching using a 6° differential, plus a loading capacity of 15 amps or 1/2 hp in 110V. Watch the optional 10 ft. lead remote bulb detector. The TEMP-H controller will activate heating equipment used to keep temperatures for both atmospheric, nutrient or propagation heating methods. Precise sensor mediates temperature by working heating equipment if it falls below the appropriate selection. Offers the very same specifications as the Coolstat and is available with remote bulbs detector.

CDM-1 CO2 Monitor

The CDM-1 is really a breakthrough in CO2 control and detection. It's a sensing device which measures the amount of CO2 in ambient airs. It uses a radical passive infrared component which samples the air once every minute and exerts a value immediately.

The passive infrared detector only determines and shows the CO_2 values in parts per million (ppm).

CO_2 is tracked continuously and displayed on a large LCD display. This allows you to maintain exact CO_2 enrichment levels without guesswork. The LCD readout shows CO_2 levels from 0 to 2,000 ppm. The screen output provides 0 to 2 VDC linear sign that may be used to interface with a computer or other auxiliary apparatus used to control CO_2 or venting gear.

The CDM-1 works on a 12VDC and is a mobile hand held unit. The CDM-1 plugs into Green Air Products Carbon Dioxide Digital Sequencer (CDDS-1) using one patch cord and becomes an automatic and programmable CO_2 management system. The built-in battery backup will force the tracking for several minutes without any auxiliary power. The CDM-1 could be immediately unplugged and removed from it is wall mount and transported to all regions of the enclosure to get immediate location checks, or by 1 greenhouse to the next.

The inner Ni-Cad battery package will recharge automatically when plugged into its power supply. The CDM-1 plugs into the Green Air Products Carbon Dioxide Digital Sequencer (CDDS-1) using one patch cord and becomes an exact and programmable CO_2 management system.

CDDS-1 Digital Controller

The CDDS-1 provides a process of accurately and automatically controlling CO_2 generating gear to assure exacting and consistent amounts. The Green Air Products CDDS-1 (Carbon Dioxide Digital Sequencer) is what transforms the CDM-1 track into a strong versatile control. The CDDS-1 supplies a simple to use set stage control which allows the user to correct CO_2 levels and length.

CO_2 values are flexible in 50 ppm increments from 0 to 2000 ppm. The length between CO 2"About" and CO2"Away" (hysteresis) can also be adjustable to 50, 150, 200 or 300 ppm differential. An LED changes colour to indicate CO_2 working status.

The CDDS-1 additionally supplies a photosensor to disable CO 2 generation during darkness periods. The CDDS-1 controller includes two regular 110V sockets on the right-hand side to operate CO_2 generating gear. The very same controls on the left-hand outlets may be utilized to operate exhaust methods for ventilation excess CO_2 accumulation in hospitals, classrooms, offices, auditoriums, labs or mushroom culture centers.

The CDM-1 and also the CDDS-1 can be found as a bundle from the CDMC-2 system. The CDMC-2 is about to work with and no additional equipment is necessary to function along with your CO 2 emitter generators or systems. For more complex applications call our advice line to observe the way the CDDC-1 may be set up in your present system.

HAR-1 Function Relay

The HAR-1 is a power relay which utilizes large amperage capability contacts to transport electricity to big fans or light systems requiring high voltage or amperage support. Used to run 110- or 240-Volt high lure equipment. It has a 30 Amp switching capability with 110 Volt triggers.

HF-1 Function Relay

The HF-1 is a high amperage relay using a built-in humidifying humidistat. Use to provide 110- or 240-Volt electricity to humidifying gear when humidity drops below set point. There is a 30 Amp switching capacity for significant load demands.

HR-1 Function Relay

The HR-1 is really a high amperage relay using a built-in outside coil heating system.

Used to provide 110 or 240 Volt electricity to heating equipment when temperature drops below place point. There is a 30 Amp switching capacity for significant load demands. A jack receptacle and inner low voltage dry connections is utilized to operate gas type heaters.

Lighting Tips Photosynthesis

Photosynthesis is the procedure in which plants use light energy to accumulate carbon dioxide from the air and convert it into chemical energy in the form of sugar. These products of photosynthesis work to nourish the plant and allow it to discharge free oxygen. Plants utilize only the range of light that's visible to your eye.

Even though the light looks white, it's really a mix of all of the colors of the rainbow. Pigments, that would be the light harvesting units of these plants, absorb specific colors of the spectrum and reflect the remainder.

Chlorophyll, the principal pigment found in photosynthesis, absorbs light in the blue and purple wavelengths in addition to from the red, leaving green the colour it reflects, as well as the plant shade we see. Photosynthesis may also happen inside, as long as the artificial light source utilized provides the essential spectrum and durability.

Broad spectrum aluminum, metal halide, and higher-pressure sodium would be the kinds of lights most commonly used for indoor climbing. Each these lights require a ballast to operate and come in many different sizes and wattage. Homegrown supplies a broad selection of grow lights that supply the essential spectrum and durability to match plants' requirements. Sun master lineup of Metal Halide Lamps was designed particularly for plant development by carefully fitting the spectrum of sunlight. Lighting is the most expansion affecting variable!

Lighting Tips

- Mylar reflects with as much as 95% efficacy
- Horizontal white paint reflects up to 80% efficacy
- Never utilize tinfoil for manifestation as it generates "hot spots"
- Utilize air cooled reflectors when heating build-up is an issue
- 15 minute time waits for halides stops "hot starts"
- Low pressure sodium lights significantly increase intensity for pennies per day
- Light movers raise growth by around 40 percent
- Halide "super" bulbs raise intensity, but maybe not your own hydro bill

- 430 watt Son Agro sodiums provide 30 additional watts of blue lighting
- Wear sunglasses when working near a H.I.D. bulb
- In case your lighting fails, do not attempt to repair it yourself, get in touch with a skilled specialist

Lighting Types.

Fluorescent

Before high intensity release light came about, indoor growers depended largely on fluorescent lighting to get the best outcomes. They're cheap, reasonably energy efficient, and many emit a broad enough spectrum of lighting for plant development. There's a vast selection of fluorescent bulbs or "tubes" accessible, and therefore they are categorized by wattage, length, and color of range array.

Indoor growers should start looking for the type especially created for crops like the vita-Lite* or Ultralume 5000*. The fittings for all these lamps are often complete with lamp holders, reflector, and built in ballast. Since the debut of H.I.D. lights, fluorescents are now mostly used for propagation and early embryonic development. The 40 watt, 48 inch, and 20 watt, 24 INCHES, would be the most usual. The intense and energy efficient H.I.D.s are now the option for maturing high-light vegetables and plants inside.

High Intensity Discharge (H.I.D.) Grow Lights

Metal halide lights were created to deliver a spectrum as near as possible to that of pure sunlight. This is coupled with their durability and energy efficiency, which makes them perfect for indoor gardening. The bulbs vary in size from 100 watt to 1000 watt with 400 watt and 1000 watt being the hottest. Plenty of blue light emitted by metal halide makes them the very best lighting for propagation and vegetative development, boosting short internodal length.

High Pressure Sodium lights don't emit as wide a spectrum as Metal Halides lights; however they have lots of benefits, especially if used along with halide. Sodiums burn brighter, and last longer, but are more energy efficient. There is more yellow/red color in the spectrum and not as blue promotes a greater flower-to-leaf ratio in flowering plants.

H.P.S. lights are broadly used in commercial greenhouses, where natural sun offers sufficient blue. A combo of those 2 lights supplies the very best balanced for indoor grow room, particularly when combined with a light mover.
430 Watt Son Agro H.P.S. bulbs that supply 30 additional watts than normal ones are now offered. This excess light at the blue end of the spectrum is excellent news for indoor growers.

If you're planning a "single lamp" grow room, then it's still possible to receive the advantages of the halide and sodium light.

High pressure sodium "conversion bulbs," especially designed to function with M.H. ballasts, are offered in 400 watt and 1000 watt models. The bulbs can readily be interchanged as required, utilizing exactly the identical ballast and fixture. The dimensions of the lighting you may need will be based on the dimensions of the growing area, and also the sort of plants you would like to grow.

High-light plants such as vegetables and herbs will need between 20 and 60 watts of light per square foot of growing space. A 400 watt metal halide works in a 3 foot by three foot area and provides 45 g per square foot, compared to 25 g per square foot in five foot by five foot grow room. A 1000 watt metal halide in a five foot by five foot area provides 40 g per sq. ft., in comparison to 20 g per square foot in a seven by seven foot grow room.

Suitable reflectors, light movers, and reflective material on walls significantly increases durability and efficacy of those lights. Most high intensity bulbs may be conducted with either 120 volts (standard house current), or 240 volts (e.g. utilized for electrical dryer).

Electricity costs are the exact same however, the latter would draw half of the amps allowing the grower to operate two times as many lamps on the identical electric circuit.

Light timers are available for voltage, but check to confirm the amperage rating on the timer surpasses that of the lights. Care should be taken when installing and utilizing H.I.D. lights. Remote ballasts must be put safely from the way where they cannot be pumped or splashed with water. Never store your ballast on the ground if it becomes wet.

Installing the fixture and reflector is straightforward. Find a stud in the ceiling close to the center of the grow area. Twist a metal hook capable of carrying 40 to 50 pounds to the stud and examine its strength. Put a 4' to 6' span of lightweight link chain onto the hook or hooks in addition to the fixture and hang the fixture on the ceiling hook at the desired height. The link chain permits you to easily increase and lower the lighting when required.

Hold the lamp close to the base and firmly, but gently, screw the bulb into the socket. Connect the timer into the power supply, plug in the power cable in the ballast to the timer which ought to be put in the "on" position. It might take around 30 minutes for your bulb to ignite and around five minutes to achieve total brightness.

Since the lamp sparks, they have a tendency to flicker and change color for many minutes. This is very normal, particularly with halide bulbs, which might seem to change color slightly during ordinary usage. If the lamp doesn't ignite after 30 or 40 minutes, then unplug it. Once the power has been disconnected, assess if:

- The bulb is screwed in all of the way
- The timer is put in the "on" position
- That wires or electrical connections are O.K.

NOTE: Don't Open the Ballast Enclosure to Assess Wiring Yourself! H.I.D. capacitors can hold a charge even after the ballast is unplugged! When these points are assessed, try out the light.

After a metal halide is switched off it requires a 15 to 20 minute "cool down" period until it can be re-started. When ample cooling time isn't permitted, a "hot start" happens, and also many "hot starts" can severely impact the degree and durability of the bulb. For the best results, substitute halide bulbs after one year of continuous use. High pressure sodium lamps need just a two to three minute "cool down" period and require only being replaced every two to three decades.

Light Movers

The most efficient method to utilize high intensity lights would be to get them moving inside the grow room. There are various benefits to this, and many of different ways it may be carried out. Transferring the lights will remove crops trend to grow toward the light source and supply light to areas which otherwise can be shaded. Considering that the light is moving, it may pass very near the plants without burning the leaves. Moving lights cover more space than static ones, reducing electricity prices and ensuring more growth.

This also allows plants to be placed much closer together, significantly increasing quality and yield. The dimensions and shape of the room will determine the sort of lighting that will suit your requirements. Lineal movers carry the light fixture gradually along a trail and back again through the light cycle. Most are just six feet, support one lamp, and therefore are recommended if the climbing area is narrow and long.

Circular movers are greatest when the width and length of this space are alike. They're intended to carry one, two, or three lights, at a 360 degree circle, ideally light a ten by ten foot area. This diameter could be reduced, but seldom extended.

Two, three and arm movers are popular, with the latter providing a whole lot lighter per square foot.

More durability implies crops can be placed much closer together, significantly increasing yields.

Benefits of using Light movers:

- More even growth over a bigger area
- Lamps could be put closer to harvest
- Increase growth by 40 percent
- Stronger plant stalks
- Counteract leaf shading
- Circular movers may move around 3 lamps

1 or 2 meter linear monitors support single lamps, and expansion kits are utilized for adding lamps.

Media and Supplies

There are many types of growing media which have been successfully employed for hydroponics and there are likely many more which have not been attempted. Some are:

1. Perlite – A volcanic stone, a grey obsidian, that's been warmed to 1,500 degrees F in a kiln and expanded. It's a lightweight porous substance that can "wick" water out of a base container of water.

2. Ceramic grow stone - A clay substance also known as Geolite, which is frequently used for aquaculture since the porous material is a great media for growing bacteria to clean water. It doesn't break down.

3. Rockwool - A material made from stone spun into a fiber like substance. A phenol based resin is added as a binder. Rockwool also tends to boost the pH of the water.

4. Pea gravel - This media is only straightforward gravel, but continues to be rated for size and contour. It's not a porous media, therefore it doesn't wick water from underneath and has to be utilized in a system which offers aeration for your water. It may be used to grow bacteria in addition to plants.

There are lots of additional kinds of media used in hydroponic systems. Some have particular benefits and pitfalls.

Sand - Lots of kinds of sands, such as shore sand, have additives already from the press, that may cause difficulties in hydroponics. But sand is a helpful media that keeps in water. It needs to be sterilized between plants.

Sawdust - Where there's an extensive timber manufacturing, sawdust might be available. The species of tree is vital, with softwoods decaying more slowly than hardwoods. Douglas fir and western hemlock work well, but red cedar is poisonous to plants. A few kinds of sawdust come from logs soaked in salt water and that is toxic to crops.

Peat - There are 3 kinds of peat: peat moss, reed sedge along with peat humus. Peat is quite acid and may lower the pH of the nutrient water. It breaks down after one or two growing seasons.

Vermiculite - This really is a volcanic mica that has been popped into a kiln. It's a calcium aluminum iron ion substance which may be compacted and shed its porosity.

Pumice - A silicon substance of volcanic source that can break down after repeated usage.

No media - There are lots of hydroponic systems which use no growth media at all. The plant is generally started in a little bit of rockwool, or a specially made collar. The plant is then put into a growing container or tube which applies nutrient water to the roots.

Selecting the Best Growing Medium

I've recorded the most favorite kinds of growing mediums under, read the facts about the overall usage, benefits and pitfalls, and particular features of the given medium that is specified.

Oasis cubes

These lightweight pre-formed cubes are used for propagation. It is a remarkably common medium used when growing from seeds or by cuttings. This product has a neutral pH and keeps water in really nicely. The cubes are intended to be a starter medium and come in 3 sizes up to 2" x 2." They may be easily transplanted into virtually any type of hydroponic system or growing (or into soil).

Coconut Fiber

Coconut fiber is quickly becoming one of the very popular

growing mediums on Earth.

In reality it may shortly become absolutely the most popular. It's the first completely "natural" growing medium that provides high performance in hydroponic systems. Coconut fiber is basically a waste product of the coconut sector, it's the powdered husks of the coconut.

There are various benefits - it preserves a bigger oxygen capacity compared to rockwool, but additionally has an exceptional water holding capacity compared to rockwool that's a true benefit for hydroponic systems which have irregular watering cycles. Coconut fiber can also be high in root stimulating hormones and it provides some protection from root diseases such as ringworm infestation.

Dutch growers have discovered that a combination of 50 percent coconut fiber and 50 percent expanded clay pellets would be the ideal growing medium. A word of warning about coconut fiber, so you have to take care once you buy it. There's a commonly available, lesser tier of coconut fiber that's full of sea-salt and it is extremely fine grained. This lower quality coconut fiber will result in unsatisfactory results when utilized in a hydroponic system.

Perlite

Great old perlite! It has been in existence for decades, mainly to be used as a soil additive to increase aeration and in draining the soil. Perlite is a mined substance, a sort of volcanic glass that if quickly heated to over 1600 deg. F. it pops up much like popcorn because of the water and leaves innumerable tiny bubbles.

Perlite is among the best hydroponic growing mediums around. Used alone or as a combination with different mediums. Perlite is often utilized with vermiculite (a 50 - 50 mix is a remarkably common medium), and can also be one of the most significant elements of soilless mixes. Perlite has great wicking action that makes it a fantastic selection for wick-type hydroponic systems.

Perlite can be relatively cheap. The largest drawback to perlite is the fact that it does not retain water well so it will dry out faster between watering. The dust in perlite is bad for your health too, so you need to wear a dust mask when handling it.

Vermiculite

Vermiculite is just another mined material. In its natural condition it looks like mica stone, but when fast heated it expands because of the creation of interlaminar steam.

Vermiculite is most often utilized along with perlite as both complement each other nicely. Vermiculite keeps moisture (roughly 200% - 300% by weight), and perlite does not, so it is possible to balance your growing medium so it retains nutrients and water well, but still provides the roots with loads of oxygen.

A 50/50 mixture of perlite together with vermiculite is a remarkably popular medium for trickle kinds of hydroponic systems in addition to ebb and flow methods. Vermiculite is cheap. The significant disadvantage of vermiculite is the fact it needs a lot of water to be utilized alone. It may suffocate the roots of crops if used directly.

Soilless Mixes

There are many sorts of soilless mixes comprising a huge range of ingredients. Most include things like Sphagnum moss, Perlite and Vermiculite. All these sorts of growing medium are often considered organic and therefore, are often used for container gardening wick systems and on-recovery drip methods.

They may be utilized in growing systems; however the majority of those combinations have some very fine particles which may clog pumps and drip emitters in case you do not use a decent filtration system.

Many soilless mixes keep water well and possess good wicking action whilst still holding a fantastic quantity of air, which makes them a great growing medium for an assortment of hydroponic and organic gardens.

Expanded Clay Pellets

This man-made item is frequently called grow stones and is a very good growing medium. It's created by coconut oil in a kiln. The interior of the clay pellets is filled with tiny air pockets (similar to lava stone) making this a type of lightweight medium (a few of those pellets float). The pellets are fantastic for ebb & flow processes or other systems which have regular watering cycles (clay pellets don't retain much water so they ought to be watered often so the roots of the plants don't dry out).

The stones are usually blended with other growing medium(s) to boost oxygen retention. Expanded clay pellets are somewhat costly, but they're among the few kinds of growing medium that's readily reusable, making them a fantastic option for the long-term. Once you harvest your crop you can wash the clay stones to remove all of the old roots and sterilize them using a 10% bleach and water mixture (one part bleach to 9 parts water). The grow stones may also be sterilized using a combination of Hydrogen Peroxide and water (use 1 or 2 tsp of 35% food grade hydrogen peroxide per gallon of water).

Sand

The Hanging Gardens of Babylon are believed to be sand-based hydroponic systems (what else could you use if you are stuck in the middle of the desert?). This is just about the very first hydroponic growing medium used, and it's still being used successfully. Sand has a propensity to pack closely together, thus cutting down the quantity of air available to the roots. That means you need to use a coarse builders sand or combine the sand with perlite or other substance that increases aeration.

Sphagnum Moss

A totally natural medium which is used as a significant ingredient in the majority of soilless mixes. Sphagnum moss is also used alone in a hydroponic system. Sphagnum moss creates a fantastic fluffy growing medium that keeps a high proportion of air and keeps water in well too. The significant issue with this growing medium is the fact it may decompose over time and you'll be able to acquire modest particles which can plug your pump and (or) trickle emitters if you're using a recovery kind of hydroponic system.

Fiberglass Insulation

I've never used fiberglass insulation but I have known many

people who have utilized it in their own hydroponic systems. There have been mixed reviews, and not one of these individuals are still using it. The most frequent criticism I have discovered is it keeps in a lot of water, not leaving space for sufficient air around the roots, which may result in issues with the plant.

I've discovered that sometimes the insulation has been treated with compounds such as fireproofing, etc., therefore if you don't want to experiment, then the Professor wouldn't advise using ceramic insulation. Air People discuss hydroponic systems which don't utilize any growing medium in any way. So far as I know, that could not be possible. The plants roots would be growing into a vacuum. This could immediately kill the plant. Air on the other hand is often utilized as a growing medium.

Aeroponic systems have the plants' roots dangling in air and are occasionally sprayed using a nutrient solution. The largest advantage to growing in air is that the roots receive all of the oxygen that they might possibly desire (roots need lots of oxygen). Another significant benefit to air is it is price (Free is difficult to beat!).

There's absolutely no disposal issues like with a few other mediums. The largest problem related to aeroponics is it is susceptibility to power failures and timer or pump failures.

There's not any buffer. The roots could begin to dry out in minutes and also the reduction of the entire harvest can come very fast.

Gravel

This growing medium has been used for decades and works nicely. The earlier hydroponic systems which were commercially available to people were gravel predicated ebb / flow (flood and drain) form systems. Gravel supplies lots of air to the roots, but does not retain water, meaning that the plants roots may dry out fast if they aren't watered enough. The other disadvantage to rosemary is its own weight, it is very heavy, and toting it around is tough.

Gravel is generally fairly cheap (based on where you reside) and simple to discover. You are able to easily reuse soil provided that you wash and sterilize nicely between plants. Once you harvest your crop, you'll be able to wash the soil to eliminate all of the old roots and sterilize them using a 10% bleach and water mixture (one part bleach to 9 parts water). The gravel may also be sterilized using a combination of Hydrogen Peroxide and water (use 1 or 2 tsp of 35% food grade hydrogen peroxide for each gallon of water).

Water

When most men and women think of hydroponics, they believe of plants with their roots wrapped in water using all the nutrients dissolved in it. This is a really common way of growing hydroponically and there are numerous kinds of systems which use water as the growing medium (deep flow N.F.T., shallow stream N.F.T. and water culture are one of the hottest). Water is a crucial component in the development of plants anyhow, so using it as the growing medium creates a great deal of sense.

Care has to be ensured when choosing a system which uses water as the sole growing medium, to make sure the plant(s) are balanced. For instance: Water-loving plants such as "Bibb" kind of lettuce does best in a water-culture system in which the plants float right on the surface with their roots dangling to the water, however the exact identical system won't work as nicely for many other crops since there's too much water and not enough oxygen. These additional plants will do better at a N.F.T. system in which more oxygen is available to the roots since the crops are suspended over the water.

Sawdust

This growing medium has had limited success.

There are numerous factors that determine how nicely sawdust will operate, most predominantly is the type of wood which the dust is created from. Some sorts of timber can give off substances that are harmful to the health of the plant(s). Another issue with sawdust is the fact it's going to decompose, which may result in problems. Sawdust also keeps in a whole lot of moisture so care has to be taken to not over water. The very best thing about sawdust is the fact it is usually free. I really don't advise using sawdust unless you're into experimentation.

Lava Rock

Lava stone has been utilized successfully for decades, it's light-weight and keeps in a decent quantity of water because it has pores and holes. It's used most frequently in ebb & flow (drain & fill) systems with regular watering cycles. Since there's a fantastic choice of first rate growing mediums accessible lava stone is used less frequently nowadays. The fall in popularity is due largely to the fact the sharp edges of this stone can lead to root damage to the plants, and in most regions of the planet it can be difficult to locate lava stone that's not chemically treated.

Super Nutrients

Secrets to Hydroponic Nutrients.

Super Veg A & B - All vital trace elements (micros) are contained for lush vegetative growth. Super Veg A & B is pH balanced to reach 6.0 to 6.5, using little to no pH up/down required. After ordering, purchase both A & B.

Super Bloom A & B - Delivers an immediate supply of nutrient uptake, in addition to the suitable follow elements (micros) to acquire substantial, multiple blooms. PH balanced, won't burn plants and increases yields radically. After ordering, purchase both A & B.

A great combination when added to the majority of nutrient solutions. Dutch scientists, following quantified research and analysis, have dried and circulated an enzyme which promotes fast plant cell division and enhanced cell wall depth. As many nutritional supplements have made many promises of improved yields and taste improvement, B-CUZZ delivers!

- Totally organic
- Entirely clean for hydroponic applications

- Descriptive booklet with instructions included with every purchase.

Dynagro is a component formula comprising all of macro, micro and trace elements.

Grow - Grow is a combination made for its vegetative growth phase.

Bloom - Bloom is a combination made for its flowering phase.

General Hydroponics the Flora series is a 3 part nutrient formulation. All three are blended in varying proportions to match plant variety and development phases. Recipes are on the bottles. General Hydroponics urges a 3-2-1 ratio for competitive plant development. At the vegetative stage, a mixture of 3 tsp. Grow, 2 tsp Micro, 1 tsp. Bloom per gallon of water and also at the flowering phase, 3 tsp Bloom, 2 tsp. Micro plus one tsp. Grow per gallon of water are recommended.

EcoGrow

Eco's formulas are buffered and pH corrected and include the right quantities off all of major and trace elements known to be needed by plants. EcoGrow is an extremely concentrated formulation balanced for the development phases of the majority of plants. EcoBloom is a low-nitrogen, high-phosphorous combination to slow vegetative development and encourage flower and fruit production. Both formulations contain considerable amounts of potassium, phosphorus, magnesium, calcium, and trace elements to keep crops vigorous and healthy during their lifespan.

The Genesis Formula

The Genesis formula included was provided for you by the very same men and women who've been bringing you quality merchandise for this business for more than ten years, those goods have shown our capacity to design the kinds of systems you need to create your work of hobby simpler, more rewarding and more enjoyable. Our goods have, and will continue to represent the best of the technology.

"The Genesis Formula" is no exception. Our chemists and horticultural employees have spent decades in the laboratory and greenhouses coordinating their attempts to invent the most comprehensive feeding program available now.

"The Genesis Formula" is advanced in its layout and composition supplying the most flexible nutrient bundle available on the market. The four component system enables flexibility to build nutrient blends to satisfy the nutritional needs of virtually any crop in any period of development.

Superthrive

A classic vitamin-hormone nutritional supplement, super thrive has been used for a long time. Its consistent outcomes as a plant stimulant and tonic are well known. Of all of the products you will see on this website, none comes more highly recommended than Super Thrive. I started using it about 25 years back, and I believe it as vital to successful bonsai farming as tools or pottery. 1 drop per gallon can help revive an ailing bonsai, improve growth and provide longer, more lasting blossoms. If you repot or root prune a bonsai, eight to ten drops per gallon utilized for a 15 minute dip will radically reduce transplant shock and losses. Additionally, it works wonders on plants.

Diamond Black

In the richest source of agronomically powerful and certified plant occupied humates. It's understood that humates function best when applied regularly throughout the growing season.

Diamond Black is the sole top notch Leonardite proven soluble throughout one season. Humates released to the plant's environment modulate the circulation and improve the transfer of nutrients. In combination with rooting media, Diamond Black will gradually break down incorporating humates into the root environment. This can be a pure mined substance and fulfills all natural criteria for crop production.

Diamond Black is a Unique kind of Leonardite comprising an exceptionally large proportion of plant energetic organic humic and fulvic acids. Diamond Black is full of organic materials beneficial to plant development and gives growers the benefits of natural organic matter in an extremely accessible and simple to use form.

- Countless University studies have shown Humates enhance plant growth and yield.
- Increases the uptake and availability of plant minerals and nutrition.
- Derived from the sole Leonardite root with recognized solubility.
- Meets guidelines for natural production.

Diamond Black could be applied to most cultivated plants such as flowers, fruits, trees, vegetables, vines and ornamentals. Use in soil, potting mixes, soilless rooting media and hydroponics.

Instructions for use

Hydroponics

Mix with hydroponic or traditional growing media like potting mixes, soil, coconut fiber (CocoTekä), clay pebbles (GroRoxÒ), rockwool or Perlite. Blend at a speed of 15030 g per liter media (2-4oz per gal).

In the plants have grown on Earth, they've adapted to use five big tools to be able to grow. These are warmth, water, oxygen, carbon dioxide, and mineral components. By these, plants may synthesize a vast assortment of organic molecules needed for life. Of these five variables, it's the mineral component requirements of crops that we aim to supply via using hydroponic or soilless civilization, and under optimal conditions of temperature and light that the growth of plants is mainly dictated by the nutrient makeup at the main zone.

As hydroponic growers and providers, it's therefore worth having a peek at what components are in fact necessary for plant development, what their objective is within the plant, and what amounts and ratios are appropriate for optimizing plant development in a selection of conditions.

Hydroponic Elements - Why we need them...

The elements required for plant growth include the following.

1Nitrogen

Nitrogen is a part of amino acids in proteins and enzymes utilized in plant cells, in addition to taste compounds and lignin, and consequently the whole plant metabolism is dependent upon a nitrogen source.

Instance of Amino Acid Comprising NITROGEN:HOOC-$(CH)n-NH_2$

Without nitrogen, plant growth stops, and deficiency symptoms quickly appear. Most evident deficiency symptoms are yellowing or purple coloration of their old leaves, thin stalks, and reduced vegetative vigor. Nitrogen is easily mobilized within the plant; therefore deficiencies appear as symptoms on the leaves that are older.

Extra nitrogen, or especially a top fructose to carbon dioxide mixture inside the plant, predisposes the plant into leafy spongy growth, generally undesirable for industrial crops and it may retard fruit collection, encourage flower abscission, and cause calcium deficiency ailments as fruits grow.

Nitrogen is provided as a nitrate from the hydroponic nutrient solution, normally from sources of calcium nitrate, and potassium nitrate (Saltpeter). Sometimes, such as under reduced light conditions, a little bit of nitrogen is provided from the ammonium form from chemicals like ammonium nitrate or ammonium phosphate, but this should be limited to less than 10 percent of the entire nitrogen content of the nutrient solution to keep balanced vegetative development and steer clear of physiological disorders regarding ammonia toxicity. Urea should not be utilized in hydroponics.

Potassium

Potassium is a vital activator of several enzymes, particularly those involved in carbohydrate metabolism. Potassium can also be accountable for the control of ion motion through water and membranes standing of stomatal apertures.

Potassium therefore has a part in controlling plant transpiration and turgor. It's usually related to plant 'quality' and is vital for effective initiation of flower buds and fruit collection. Because of this the amount of potassium in nutrient options is raised as plants enter a 'reproductive' stage, and as plants grow into reduced light levels, so as to keep nutrient equilibrium in alternative.

Symptoms of potassium deficiency are usually, scorched spots involving the margins of older leaves, as well as normally low energy and susceptibility to fungal infection. Compounds such as berries may practically double their uptake of potassium through fruiting. A perfect source of potassium for indices is monopotassium phosphate, with potassium nitrate.

Potassium sulphate may be utilized as an additive to improve potassium levels without impacting nitrogen or phosphorous. Potassium chloride ought to be used sparingly if at all, to prevent excess pollution levels in the solution.

Phosphorous

The energy usage procedure within plants is based on bonds involving phosphate molecules - energy is stored and published by the chemical adenosine triphosphate (ATP).

The phospholipid lecithin, is a part of every living cell.

Phosphorus is involved from the bonding structure of nucleic acids DNA and RNA. Deficiency of phosphate appears as a dull green coloration of these elderly leaves followed by brown and purple colors as the foliage dies.

Root growth becomes limited as phosphorous deficiency happens, as a result of glucose production and translocation being impeded. The chief supply of phosphate in hydroponics is monopotassium phosphate, though restricted quantities of ammonium phosphate can occasionally be added. Compounds like calcium superphosphate ought to be prevented. Small quantities of phosphorous are also provided by using phosphoric acid for pH control.

Magnesium

Magnesium is the fundamental ion of the chlorophyll molecule, and consequently has a main function in the mild collecting mechanism of this plant and the creation of plant sugars through photosynthesis.

Magnesium can be a co-factor from the energy utilization process of respiration from the plant.

Magnesium deficiency first occurs as yellowing of the leaves between veins around the mature regions of the plant, even though under worse shortages the indicators can propagate towards the more recent growth. Magnesium deficiency may also occur during periods of low light intensity or heavy harvest loading and if excessive levels of potassium have been supplied in the nutrient solution.

The primary, probably universal supply of magnesium for indices is calcium sulphate (Epsom salts). Though limited use is occasionally made from magnesium nitrate, it's seldom an economical choice. Soil fertilizer salts magnesium phosphate or calcium ammonium phosphate aren't appropriate.

Calcium

Calcium is deposited in plant cell walls during their formation. It's also needed for the stability and functioning of cell membranes. Calcium deficiency is not uncommon in hydroponic plants, and is evident as tip burn in lettuce, and blossom end rot in tomatoes.

Magnesium is nearly totally immobile in the plant, because after deposited in cell walls it can't be moved. Thus the lack occurs in the latest growth. Calcium transport depends upon active transpiration; therefore calcium deficiency happens most frequently under conditions in which transpiration is limited, i.e. warm humid or moist conditions are often known as "calcium strain" periods.

Increasing salt material in solution is not likely to enhance uptake, and in reality, reducing CF is a method to boost calcium uptake in many species by improving the uptake of water.

Calcium is provided by default in many formulations throughout using calcium nitrate. Extra calcium can be offered by calcium chloride.

Sulfur

Sulfur is used chiefly in sulfur-containing proteins utilizing the amino acids cysteine and methionine. The vitamins thiamine and biotin, as well as the cofactor coenzyme A, all use sulfur, and thus this component also plays an integral part in plant metabolism. Sulfur deficiency in hydroponics is infrequent, usually since sulfur is present in sufficient quantities through using sulfate salts of another significant elements, especially potassium and magnesium, and plant demands for the component are reasonably flexible inside rather a broad selection. Where it happens, sulfur deficiency shows up as an overall yellowing of the whole foliage, particularly on new growth.

Iron

Iron is a part of proteins inside plant chloroplasts, in addition to electron transport proteins in the photosynthetic and respiration chains. Deficiency happens on the newest leaves, and also appears first as a result on the leaves between veins, and the entire leaf becomes light yellowish, even white, and finally with necrotic (dead) spots and twisted leaf margins.

Iron has to be provided as chelated Iron EDTA, EDDHA or even EPTA in hydroponics, instead of sulphate. Iron is the component most vulnerable to precipitation at large (>7) pH, therefore pH control to under pH 6.5 is imperative to keep iron as an option in hydroponics.

Manganese

Manganese catalysis the splitting of water molecules at photosynthesis, with the discharge of oxygen. It's a co-factor at the creation of chlorophyll and the respiration and photosynthetic systems. Manganese deficiency appears as a dull gray look followed by yellowing of the most recent leaves between the veins, which generally stay green. Areas of dead tissue become evident on affected leaves.

Manganese is provided by manganese sulfate, or manganese EDTA in hydroponics. The type of manganese in these types of fertilizers may vary widely between different resources, as a result of these variables as distinct 'water of crystallization' ($MnSO_4 \cdot nH_2O$), also distinct chelating agents and raw components too as production processes. Manganese, like iron, is very available to plants at high pH.

Zinc

Zinc contributes to the formation of chlorophyll, as well as the creation of this plant hormone auxin. It's an integral part of many plant enzymes. Zinc deficiency seems as noticeable and interveinal chlorosis of older leaves of the harvest, and retarded stem growth. Zinc is provided by zinc sulfate, or zinc EDTA in hydroponics.

Boron

Boron is required chiefly for cell division in plants, and deficiencies seem like calcium deficiencies, with stem cracking and passing of the shoot apex being the most important symptoms. Boron is provided as either borax (sodium borate) or lactic acid in hydroponic production.

Copper

Copper is required in small quantities as a part in many critical enzymes. Toxicity occurs more frequently than a lack of aluminum in hydroponics. Copper sulfate is most frequently used, though copper EDTA may also be utilized in nutrient solutions.

Silica

Lately silicates have been reported to enhance the growth of several plants. When available, protein has been integrated into the main system, and seems to increase nutrient uptake, enhancing the capacity of plants to generate higher yields. Silicates also have been implicated in improving pollination, in addition to providing increased structural advantage of stalks and a few resistances to foliar diseases.

It is noteworthy, that one of the 110 or so understood elements, many more are most likely to be implicated in plant development.

Chromium, nickel, titanium, cobalt, iodine, selenium, ginseng and many others are reported to have a role in certain species of plants.

Hydroponic Nutrient Basics

There are several significant elements to choose when buying additives for hydroponic nutrient formulae:

1. The salt has to be completely soluble in water, so the salt shouldn't contain additives or sterile fillers, or elements (for instance, insoluble sulphates and phosphates) that while useful for soil fertilizer are improper in hydroponics.

2. Contents of sodium, chloride, ammonium and organic nitrogen, or components not needed for plant expansion ought to be minimized under ordinary usage. These components if used by plants have a tendency to collect in recirculating hydroponic nutrients to the extent the measured CF comprises a higher percentage of lipoic salts.

3. The salt shouldn't react with different elements in precisely the exact same combination to generate insoluble salts, and it shouldn't radically alter the pH of the nutrient solution.

4. For industrial use, the fertilizer root has to be economical. There's not any use using costly fertilizer additives when a less costly source is totally adequate.

———

Why Not TDS Meters?

An alternative to fix the issues using CF for a dimension might appear to be to utilize 'TDS' or total dissolved solids as a measure of nutrient solution strength, and when 'TDS Meters' actually did so, it might address the issues. Nevertheless a 'TDS' meter is a 'CF' meter using different calibration and screen.

It only measures electric conductivity, and actually is not as accurate due to the assumptions made concerning the salt cosmetics of this alternative. Many suppose sodium chloride and also have a predetermined conversion factor (e.g. 70ppm a CF unit) that can't be corrected for different alternative formulas. TDS meters that could be calibrated for various formulations are a much better choice, but nevertheless are measuring CF in fact.

CF Effects on Plant Growth

If we presume that in the CF is a measure of the potency of a nutrient solution, this has a substantial influence on the development of plants, irrespective of the mineral material of this solution. Osmosis describes the behavior of ions in solution if separated by a semi-permeable membrane, as such as in the port of cells and nutrient solution.

The focus of ions on either side of the membrane determines the net flow of electrons through the membrane, like ions are more concentrated in alternative than in root cells and the cartilage allows the transmission of ions, subsequently ions will tend to flow to the roots. This procedure is called 'passive' transportation or diffusion, and can be aided by the stream of water from the transpiration stream of this plant. In reality, root cells often maintain very high 'osmotic potentials' but reduced levels of ions that attract ions and water to the roots.

Favorable Tips on Formulation and Feeding-Operation Cycle

There are two ways to secure the magical mix and the ideal ratios. You purchase pre-formulated nourishment or you invent in them independently. In the first choice, all you need to do is mix a typical quantity prescribed by the producers of the focus with water. The next choice though is that the more cost-efficient and powerful because your mixtures will probably be based on what your own crops will require. Whichever you opt for, there are factors which you have to remember like the pH level or acidity material of this formulation because the capacity of the roots to absorb the nutrition will rely on it. Below are a few friendly ideas you may research and consider:

1. Keep your formulations' pH level in the very best range to your favourite plants, that is 5.8 to 6.5. A level of pH at 1 is acidic, at 7 impartial, and 14 basics. You are able to assess the pH level using a chemical test kit which requires replenishment since the substances are consumed or via electronic techniques such as pencils with LCD monitors which are dipped into the solution.

2. Fix the pH level if needed. This may be accomplished by using distilled vinegar. A complete mix or balance one of phosphoric, nitric, and sulfuric acids is equally

important particularly they optimize the possible advantages your plants may derive from nutrients like phosphorous, nitrogen, and sulfur. To be able to boost the pH foundation you'll be able to use potassium hydroxide and sodium hydroxides. It is possible to use soda as an ingredient representative also.

3. Use alternate purification methods in feeding the nutrients into the plants apart from the ones which are currently in practice. These systems which are most frequently utilized are aeroponics, constant flow alternative culture, static alternative culture, flooding and drain sub-irrigation, passive sub-irrigation, high irrigation, ultrasonic irrigation, and deep-water culture. Option feeding techniques incorporate using coconut fibers which are pre-treated. There are lesser sodium and potassium contents and those extremely abundant with calcium and magnesium, which can be both very helpful in raising or enhancing the development of your plants.

4. Change the nutrient solution every 2 weeks. Eliminate the old solution in the reservoir and then clean the equipment with warm water to kill any lingering bacteria that might have been collected.

5. Recycle the older solution. Rather than throwing it out, use it to water the crops.

6. Keep the level of this water reservoir. Make certain to test it on a daily basis because water evaporates faster through warm times.

7. Don't underestimate the feeding. An excessive amount of nutritional supplement could result in the passing of your precious crops and would mean fantastic losses in your part.

8. Dissolve the powdered alternative before you put it from the water in the reservoir. If you're using concentrated liquids, then it's better to blend them rather than directly placing them in the water also.

9. Cease nutrient feeding your plants at least seven days before their harvest. Continue the water feeding however.

10. Oxygenate your own water. It's possible to age tap water to 3 times by putting it in a container.

Ventilation: Handling Heating

Due of the susceptibility of crops to weather fluctuations, it's crucial that you handle heat nicely in your own garden. Some states have only two seasons: dry and wet; and among these is Australia. The dry seasons will normally last for six months in which temperatures are reduced.

Throughout the rainy seasons, which generally requires a span of six months also, there's too much rain and the temperature is elevated because of increased humidity from the air.

For hydroponic growers such as you, these weather changes can pose a whole lot of challenges as with using artificial light, organic temperature is increased by the warmth exuded from the artificial lighting. The more wattage you utilize, the more increased heat is created. Too much heat can ruin your favorite plants before they flower or grow.

What You Can Do

There are several things which may be done to control heat to increase or reduce it. You need to find out how to take care of heat since they could be too low or too high. When it's too low, your crops will perish with cold; and with it too low their leaves will probably coil in and finally perish. These are a few basic things you can do:

- Utilize air-conditioners or port systems to modulate airflow and so the warmth of your hydroponics space. If air conditioners are too pricey for you concerning electricity use, then make a port system. The most frequent port systems are the ones which create hot air flow in the ceiling of the planting area to a different area.

Other vent systems have been set up to dissipate the air through the chimney, walls, as well as roofs. You are able to use simple equipment like bathroom fans to function as exhausts.

- Monitor the humidity and temperature of your hydroponic growth region by means of a thermometer. Produce a system which may clear the heat up in five minutes and at cycles of twenty-five minutes when the synthetic lights have been turned on. You need a timer and fan for this kind of system.
- Establish a system that's based on your thermostat. It is going to automatically turn a fan or air-conditioner on if a particular temperature or heating level is attained and will switch off the cooling gear once the amount decreases at least 4 degrees Celsius.
- For internal air motion functions, oscillating fans can perform. It helps carbon dioxide flow and at precisely the exact same time will keep the mounting down humidity within the garden. This is essential to be completed as a way to decrease prevalence of plant ailments because of fungus and absorb the moisture inside the room.
- To prevent declines in temperatures, which generally occurs at night or any time your artificial light is off, you need to set up a propane heater that's set to coordinate with a timer or thermostat. In case you choose to use a

thermostat, then set it to discover a temperature drop below 20 degrees Celsius and then on the heater and also then turn it off after the heat level is at 30 degrees Celsius. In addition, this system will offer your plants higher sources of carbon dioxide, and this can be a vital component in photosynthesis.

- Setup of a thermo-hygrometer. You can change it on for a span of twenty five hours or more. It will give you accurate observation of the degrees of temperature and humidity.

Lighting: Fluorescent and HPS

Lighting is required by your favorite plants in your hydroponic garden for photosynthesis and as signs of weather and seasons. With hydroponics lighting systems, you can control time and length of the exposure of the plants to heat for purposes of standardizing the photosynthesis cycles. With them you can also simulate the seasons to be able to promote them to blossom and expand the growing season so you would like year-round source of your favorite fruits and plants. Imagine that in seasons of winters, then your crops would nevertheless continue to grow and flourish. If individuals are supplied fats, plants get them out of light. With artificial light, your favorite plant can grow as large as six feet tall in 3 or four weeks.

Great Artificial Lighting Systems

Your favorite hydroponic plant will certainly blossom to its fullest capacity and provide you the highest quality and amount possible through the subsequent artificial lighting methods:

- Fluorescent and LED (or light emitting diodes) are used during the point where the seedlings of your crops are beginning to grow.

- Metallic halide (or MH) and higher pressure sodium (HPS) systems will be ideal for the flowering phase.

Fluorescent Bulbs Described More

Fluorescent bulbs are perfect for seedlings, and due to their low intensity, they will need to be set closer to the plants. They ought to be retrieved at eight to fifteen inches in the plants. They have the following advantages:

- Enhancement of the health and strength of seedlings or cuttings
- Superior root growth
- Optimize the plant reaction concerning photosynthesis

Unveiling Metal Halide Bulbs

They supply your hydroponic garden abundant green and blue spectrum lighting, which is vital in the development of those plants. With them, you may be ensured that your plant's foliage growth will be maximized and they'll grow compact or sturdy. In contrast to incandescent and fluorescent bulbs, they're best for its flowering period due to their brightness is 125 lumens, which can be very immense in contrast to 18 lumens of incandescent and 39 lumens of fluorescent bulbs. They are both effective and successful through the vegetative and flowering phases.

HPS Bulbs in Their Very Best

High pressure sodium bulbs are thought to be best for its enhancement of their budding and flowering procedures of your favorite plants since they emit light of their crimson and yellow spectrum. To put it differently, they're bulbs emitting light which closely reproduces natural light. Many users prefer them throughout the flowering period of the hydroponic garden.

Fundamental Lighting Tips You Must Follow

No matter your favorite system is on the hydroponic garden, you shouldn't neglect to perform the following so as to make the most of your plants' health, growth, and reproduction:

- For 2 months, always expose the young plant or seedlings to light. When in plant phase, illuminate them 22 hours daily; and if they're lively, keep them cooled for no more than twelve hours every day.

- Maintain the light near the crops, but do not permit them to touch the leaves. When the borders of the leaves pops, it usually means they are overheated.

- Throughout the plant stage, use bulbs which emit red or blue on the spectrum. Metal halide lamps offer the blue lighting; and fluorescent, the reddish light.

- Minimum mild exposure is 20 watts per foot. You can go considerably higher, but not overly high or your crops can fry instead of too low since they may droop.

- Attach the lamps into the roof to manage you flexibility. Since the plants grow taller, you can raise the bulbs higher.

- Utilize reflectors to ensure uniform lighting among all your plants. The ones which don't get as much light as others might grow disfigured, taller, and thinner.

- Program and layout a daily light cycle. If you don't do so, your crops will grow badly. And if you wake them up when they have been used to a dark period of the day, then they'll be traumatized and may turn out to be sick.

- Paint your walls, roofs, as well as flooring white to supply increased light reflection ability of your area. Brighten the times of your favorites and also make them feel loved and cared for.

Clones: Increasing the Success Rate of Your Hydroponic Gardening

Cloning is simply taking a cutting out of your plant and putting it with different cuttings in a different container or pot. Make certain the clone you select comes from plants. When properly taken cared for, they will end up older plants which are exact copies of the source or rootal plants. It's a technique that will surely help you in controlling the level of your crops seeds, and their fruits. Even the clones grow faster than the ones that are raised from seeds, and this is going to make your time usage more effective.

Useful Suggestions to Boost Your Success Rates

Clones are extremely effective tools in replicating your plants in your hydroponic job. You have to take additional care, however, to be sure of success or you will only be wasting time, energy, and money on these. All these are helpful tips which might assist you:

- Just clone plants which are healthy, well developed, and also have improved flowering abilities.
- Take more cuttings than you need to plant so you will get a larger selection of alternatives. Pick the very best among them.
- Before shooting a cutting, remove the nitrogen in the root plant by feeding it completely with water that's pH adjusted and with no fertilizer or nutrient to get at least

2 and maximum of 3 times. In the event you neglect to do it, you may impede the development of the roots of the clones.

- Carefully pick the sites you will utilize with your own clones. It's possible to use cubes which are pre-formed and include holes to match to your cuttings.

- You need to cut holes at the top of the medium which is the identical size or circumference as the stalks of your clones.

- Take additional care once you cut. Remember to sterilize your cutting-edge gear when you proceed with the cloning procedure since you could infect the mother plant. Be certain that if you cut, you get it done fast so as to prevent air from being taken into the stem.

- The clone must be between three and half inches --no more and no less. There should be a single leaf inter-node and when at all possible, two inter-nodes.

- Set the cuttings in a misting dome where they'll be moisturized two to 3 times a day. Keep them well ventilated also by cutting little holes in the cover of the dome. Keep their temperature at 72 degrees to 80 degrees Fahrenheit.

- Utilize double tube fluorescents that emit white light--both warm and cold. Keep them near the clones in a distance of a couple of inches. In the event you use an artificial light system which uses metal halide bulbs or higher-pressure sodium lamps, then maintain the cuttings at an interval of a couple of feet when the light source is between 175 and 400 watts. When the bulbs' wattage is a million, maintain them at a distance of four feet. Keep the cuttings illuminated at least two hours every day.

- Water the clones each 2 times with distilled water with nourishment. If the outside temperature is high, you can water them once each day. Don't make the error of submerging or placing them because the stalks will become rotten or decayed.
- In about a week, check out the clones. If you see they have begun to root, stop the misting or synthetic moisturizing procedures. Should they've properly rooted, remove the plants and dome them.

Harvest: Curing the Proper Way

The Ideal Time to Harvest Your Own Hydroponic Garden

In case you have attained as much as it simply means one thing: you've been effective with your plants' growth and flowering phases. You've won on the challenges of hydroponic gardening and triumphantly circumvented the adversities of increasing your cherished fruits.

The typical harvest period is after eight to twelve months of flowering. You have to remember they are best chosen when trichomes manufacturing or THC level is at a max. A sign of this is when at least a third of the pistils or hairs have turned from white to dark like brown or red in colour. Use a magnifying glass to track the pistils. Don't over-wait though until each the pistils are dim since it is going to reduce the value of your crops.

Quality and potency are two non-parallel goals in harvesting. If the prior is your target, you need to harvest if the THC level creation is at its maximum and your chosen plants will weigh lower but their quality will be a whole lot better. If the latter is the goal, then crop them after all of the pistils are dim.

Drying to Boost Quality

After harvest, you've got to divide the leaves out of the buds. The following step is to dry and heal them. You should remember your buds and leaves make a bad taste in your mouth and also have unpleasant odor if they're used or consumed directly after harvest. They need to be dried to extract or evaporate the water out of them. The healing step will finish the drying process and totally change the leaves of your plants to bearers of great dreams and magical. Below are a few things you have to do if drying your crops:

- Hang them in an environment that's dry, dark, and cool. Maintain the temperature at 20 degrees Celsius or 68 degrees Fahrenheit. Too much light and heat will ruin their quality.

- Don't directly deal with the plants. Avoid damaging the quality of the buds, heads, and leaves by contaminating them with grime or the perspiration of your palms.

- Separate the big branches and broader leaves in order that you can provide better drying vulnerability to the branches and thinner leaves.

- Maintain the drying branches at a distance of half a foot. If they're too close to one another, your crops may attract mold; and if they're too far from one another, they'll be dried quicker than what's needed. Both scenarios will cause the reduction of effectiveness and a drop in quality.

- The typical drying interval is different between a week and three months. To assess if your crops have correctly dried already, take some branches and then bend them. If they'd snap at an angle of 90 degrees or not, it usually means your plants are dried . If they won't, then you've got to allow them to dry more.

The Magic of Curing

Curing is a significant process in your hydroponic gardening job since it is accountable for changing your crops to marketable goods with a quality that's of high commercial values.

Just be sure before you do some of the actions associated with treatment, you've correctly dried them. Watch these tricks and for certain, you would like the victory which you've longed for:

- Put your plants in air-tight containers. Store the containers in an area where the temperature is stabilized at 20 degrees Celsius. Make certain no light will permeate the space since it will harm the item.
- Any remaining moisture from the contents of these sealed containers will surely vanish and cling to the inner surface of these containers. Gently open the lids and allow the additional moisture to escape. Do this through the very first week with an interval of 24 hours for approximately a span of half an hour. During the next week, then repeat the procedure with an interval of 48 hours. Repeat this at the next week along with other weeks if needed until all condensation is eliminated.
- Watch out for potential decay due to an excessive amount of moist. Signs of mold include a smell that's the exact same to that of compost and grass clippings that are fresh.
- Maintain the dried plants which aren't so green anymore in air-tight containers which needs to be set in a spot with a temperature of twenty degrees Celsius.

- Maintaining them in a refrigerator would help a great deal in preventing exposure to pollution, warmth, and light that might result in erosion of quality and shortening of shelf life. Maintain them untouched for many months or weeks.

Prevention and Eradication

The prevention and eradication of bugs are among the most crucial concerns among hydroponic scientists and planters in agriculture. With the arrival of scientific studies and methods of analyzing bugs, contemporary science has developed innovative procedures to offset the development and block the presence of bugs. The latest and most effective is biological pest management. This way is straightforward and just requires that favorable bugs have been introduced into the environment to offset the harm of damaging bugs.

The Predator Bugs You Must Destroy on Your Hydroponic Garden

At different phases, your plant might suffer from other types of germs. You need to be knowledgeable about these so you will understand how to stop and ruin them. Throughout the rise of the seedling of the plants the next bugs can infest them and kill or harm them.

- Cutworms: Larvae of the turnip moths. They feed on the leaves, stems, and buds of young seedlings.
- Hemp flea beetles: They are quite small jumping beetles that eat the leaves of seedlings.
- Crickets: They're detrimental to people but quite deadly to plants since they feed on buds and leaves, particularly the ones which are just in their early growth.

If your plants grow taller and create wider leaves and if they also begin to blossom, these bugs will certainly provide you plenty of headaches unless avoided.

- Spider mites: They're extremely small and almost imperceptible to your eyes. They reproduce at an extremely quick speed; and before you know it, they've ruined your entire harvest. The evidence of their existence is typically the occurrence of dead spots on the leaves. When they've powerfully infested your crops, the leaves will turn yellow, virtually the color of bronze.
- Aphids: They're also known as plant eaters and are extremely prevalent in temperate zones. They feed on the sap of plants and therefore are likely to harm the blooms even before they blossom.
- Whiteflies: They seem like fruit flies but are somewhat more devious since they chew on the leaves and blossoms of the beloved plants.
- Leafhoppers: Taxonomy smart, they're like grasshoppers just fairly smaller. They flourish on green leaves.

Other bugs which could infect the stems, stalks, and roots include the following:

- European corn borers: They are usually seen in corn; however they also have been observed to harm your favorite plants' stems.
- Hemp borers: the majority of the time they infest fruits, but they also love the stalks of green produce.
- Weevils: They prefer dry plants or surroundings. They're harmful destroyers of stems and stalks.
- Root maggots: They feed on the roots of crops. They hurt the osmosis capacity of their roots.
- Termites and ants: Self-organized insects which feed on the roots and therefore are capable of adapting to whatever environment the crops are in.
- Fungus gnats: They're dark smaller flies with brief lives but barbarous influence on the roots they infest.

The Most Effective Solutions

There are lots of accessible solutions that can help you eliminate and protect against insect infestation of your favorite plants. Five of those techniques are shown below:

- Biological pest management via the use of a valuable or little animal that eats the bugs which harm your crops. They restrain adult pests and ruin their youthful eggs, and larva. Some instances have been predatory mites to counter rainwater mites, nematodes such as weevils, lace wing for aphids, and parasitic wasp for white flies.

- Bio-best spray which come in spray or concentrates cans. All you need to do is spray it onto the affected leaves.
- Sticky plates which act as the alarm systems, plus they draw bugs due to their yellow colour.
- Plant protects that emit scents which are insect repellants.
- Neem oil which hurts the nervous systems of germs.

Sound Preventive Steps

Eradication could be very pricey, and prevention may cost you nothing in any respect. Listed below are a few suggestions you might consider stopping bug infestations in your growth room:

- Consistently clean your equipment before and after utilizing them.
- Maintain appropriate drainage to ensure cleanliness of the area.
- Don't overwater since the unused water can turn into the harbor of bugs.
- Quarantine infected crops to stop others from being apprehended also.

The Perpetual Harvest: Sea of Green Techniques

These techniques involve the harvesting of batches of little plants that grow early. They refer to this procedure in hydroponic gardening in which smaller crops have been increased over shorter periods of time rather than growing few large plants during a lengthy time period. With hydroponics in which the environment is controlled by light to venting, it's likely to begin a batch in a previous period, and as they grow, a different batch is begun.

This system contributes to a yearlong growing and harvesting cycle. Another method of accomplishing this is beginning all of the crops together and growing a green canopy in which you allow your plant be harvested more frequently than before. Taller plants will be harvested in the very best first without uprooting them. Since the plant grows more, the sooner reduced degree becomes the top that's prepared for harvest.

Here Are a Few Tips for Powerful Hydroponic Gardening and Hydroponic Growing Systems:

Ensure that you have the correct light, humidity, temperature and location in your Home Hydroponic Gardening place.

The positioning of your garden needs to maintain a high traffic location in your house so as to guarantee the most quantity of carbon dioxide from the air. Optimum temperatures should be between 65 degrees and 75 degrees Fahrenheit. Median humidity is suitable.

As soon as you have chosen your place, you'll need grow lights, a timer, Hydroponic grow boxes, along with other hydroponic supplies so as to establish your hydroponic gardening strategy. Move as large or as little as you have space for.

Your grow lights are an integral element of your home-based gardening system. You are going to need to start your young plants with around 8 hours of sun every day for some time. Take care to not use a lot of grow lights or a lot of hours of sun since over exposure can damage your plants. If you would like to experiment with light levels, present more light gradually.

A key to successful hydroponic gardening is both getting and keeping the very best equilibrium in the nutritional formulation utilized to nourish and keep your plants. PH levels are of fantastic significance.

Plant roots have to be kept within this nutritional formula so as to generate healthy vegetables, flowers, and herbs.

Beginners should probably get among those ready formulas available on the market. The components must include: calcium nitrate, potassium, nitrate, potassium phosphate, and calcium sulfate.

You'll also need sulfates, aluminum, iron, zinc, oleic acid, and ultimately magnesium chloride. Finest use of this formula could be daily for two days to get young plants, then each seven days after your Hydroponically grown plants reach maturity. Luckily, there are lots of fine hydroponic providers that could simplify the nutrition for you. You also have to make optimum absorption rate on your crops. This may be carried out with appropriate air flow using an air hose and pump.

Gardeners are discovering Home Hydroponic Gardening is a fantastic way of growing year-round plants. Imagine fresh red yummy berries in December. New herbs all year around for seasoning your own meals. With the bonus of new exquisite flowers year-round.

Important Details Concerning the Hydroponics Garden

Before you begin with your own garden, you have to understand a couple of things.

Otherwise, you run the risk of investing a great deal of money and time, rather than getting the return you had hoped for. I n the end, there is much more to gardening than simply purchasing the ideal hydroponics nutrients and lots of additional supplies. You need to discover the right installation for your circumstance. There is a good deal of possibility in hydroponic gardening, however it is not necessarily straightforward. Let us take a peek at a few of the most frequent issues you may expect to encounter along with your hydroponics garden.

Cost - It may be very expensive to establish your hydroponics garden. The gear simply to begin necessitates some true investment. The expense of the garden goes in the very long term, obviously, but you need to know what it is going to take to put up things. Do not get into this kind of gardening with the misunderstanding that it is cheap. Even though a hydroponic garden frequently generates better than a soil garden, it is less expensive.

Maintenance - You will need to carry out regular maintenance if you would like your garden to function properly. Unlike soil gardens, that do things by themselves, your hydroponics systems will melt with no regular maintenance.

How long are you going to need for upkeep? It is dependent upon the sort of system you purchase. Most will need at least a modest daily care, which may lead to travel issues. It can be tough to discover a garden-sitter.

Sickness - Hydroponics Gardens have a lesser prospect of particular varieties of ailments, particularly in the event that you practice careful management. That does not mean they are free of illness, however. In the end, all of the plants share the exact same nutrient solution. In case a waterborne disease gets, it could spread really quickly via your hydroponics systems. Even though this isn't troublesome for gardens which are carefully maintained free from contamination, it can be a huge issue if you allow yourself to get cluttered.

Knowledge - You Need to have more background knowledge to efficiently grow a hydroponics garden. Soil based gardens are somewhat easier for novices. It may be a great deal of fun to acquire this understanding, but it will require some work. Remember - you cannot grow every plant in this manner, and you have to understand a lot about what you're able to grow. Each plant has distinct light, nutrient, and maintenance requirements.

Do these drawbacks mean you cannot have your hydroponics garden? Not if you have some opportunity to learn what you will need to understand first. As you do need some basic tools, there are loads of excellent gardens out there which could do the job for you. Whether you would like a rotary Volksgarden kind of system or a standard hydroponic garden, you can get things growing!

Hydroponic Tent Benefits

From farmers to amateur home horticulturalists, hydroponics has gained immense popularity because of the many advantages. Hydroponic tents play an essential part in the fast cultivation of plants and thus it's compulsory for the growers that perform the indoor hydroponics gardening to use the hydroponic tents. Hydroponic tents end in lush and healthy plants.

Moreover with the assistance of these grow tents you need less time and less space to grow the vegetables and plants. They're simple to establish and can be found at inexpensive rates. Additionally with the assistance of hydroponic tents you may control the plants' surroundings such as the humidity and root zone temperature.

Hydro tents can be found in various styles and sizes. Hydroponics tents can also be ecofriendly and will save you lots of cash since a lesser quantity of water is called for in the hydroponic methods when compared with water employed in the traditional gardening. The interior walls of the tent radiate the light whereas the dark walls onto the exteriors absorb the warmth.

Thus if you're contemplating hydroponic gardening afterward hydroponic tents are must-haves. These tents shield the young plants entirely and assist in growing healthy crops, without needing direct sunshine. They operate like mini greenhouses. By employing the hydroponic tents you can control the conditions where the plants grow. These tents end with the plants in pristine quality.

Hydroponic grow tents assist in providing the ideal air for the plants to grow and the grower is readily able to restrain the plants' temperature and humidity. Thus hydroponic growth is the ideal means to nourish plants. People that are new to this subject can choose the smaller grow tents so you can see if you're able to grow the vegetables and plants efficiently.

Hydroponic tents prove to work in safeguarding your seedlings from direct sunlight or strong winds. Young plants when they're in their growing phase require a sufficient quantity of moisture, consequently the hydroponic tents are adept at trapping moisture that in turns demonstrates it is beneficial for your seedlings to grow efficiently.

The lights, namely large Pressure Sodium Lights, as well as the Metal Halide Grow Lights, fit perfectly in a grow tent and can create lots of warmth, hence providing a nourishing environment for your sickly plants. Hydroponic grow tents aren't heavy and can easily be mobile and so they may be moved easily with no sort of hassles. Hydroponic grow tents would be the cheapest way to grow plants indoors.

Prior to choosing an appropriate grow tent contemplate a number of the significant items like the dimensions of the tent that fits comfortably within your room, air intake vents, etc.

To be able to purchase the tents it is also possible to take ideas from the seasoned gardeners who've been in this area for quite a while. Thus it's advised to perform a comprehensive study if you're searching for a grow tent. Consequently grow tents play a very important role in controlling the interior growing surroundings of the vegetables and plants. You can search the Net since there are various sites which provide information on grow tents.

Hydroponic Gardening - Frequent Problems Encountered by Beginners

It's not hard to get your hydroponic system set up. The majority of the Hydroponic Gardening guides, particularly those for beginners, include a part on build-it-yourself hydroponic systems. They supply a parts list, a tools list, and easy step-by-step education about the best way best to construct your own growing system.

But after the Hydroponic unit is in operation, rather frequently, the novices will detect problems, some might not be readily solved after the machine has been built. As a result, as you're planning to create your hydroponic system, it's always a good idea to understand the problems normally encountered by novices. They might affect your needs or the design of your hydroponic system.

The followings are several of those cases.

Problem#1

There's a concern on exactly how much nutrition should be poured across the aggregate.

Because for all those hydroponic systems utilizing a "light proof" container concept, you won't have the ability to see via the containers down throughout the aggregate. So it's extremely tricky to evaluate the quantity or degree of nutrient solution. With this vulnerability, the crops may probably be killed by either under or overfilling.

The workable alternatives may be put a visual indication showing the nutrient solution amount or water detectors for an automatic method.

Problem#2

The next difficulty is how frequently to pour nutrient within the aggregate. If you merely adhere to the period for your usual home plants grown in soil, for instance, three to four times every week, you'd likely kill your hydroponic plants. For instance, due to the broader air gap from the aggregate when compared with soil, the nutrient solution will have a tendency to evaporate in the aggregate considerably faster than water from soil. So in general, you would have to provide nutrient for your plants at least once every day.

The simpler the system, the more often you'll need to include nutrient solution. The period could be anywhere from one to four times each day based on many factors, such as temperature, light, humidity, type and dimensions of your plants, and also the size of your container. This usually means you can't even go away for a weekend or your hydroponic plants will start to suffer.

The answers for this problem are to find somebody to "feed" the crops for you whenever you're away for over a day or to make your hydroponic system automatic.

Problem#3

A third issue involves appropriate aeration (or distribution of oxygen or air) for your plants' roots. This area generally isn't a concern for soil gardening in the garden since worms do this function. In some hydroponic systems, especially those utilizing PVC pipes with holes drilled for crops, too frequently the roots clog up the waterways and aeration in the root canal might run into an issue.

Various systems will have various methods for supplying suitable aeration, for cases, using pumps, elevated platforms or special aggregate acceptable for hydroponics.

Simple Issues?

To some folks, these issues appear to be an issue of common sense. But if you're a newcomer to the soil-less gardening notion and without going through the authentic exercise after, you're very likely to find a great deal of trivial issues like those mentioned previously if you don't plan well.

Read More Before Implementing

Therefore, before constructing your own hydroponic system, it's almost always a great idea to start with reading hydroponics beginner's guides. Take time to read and completely comprehend the concept in addition to the advantages and disadvantages of different types of hydroponic systems. As for me, I suggest reading at least three novels because different novels focus on various aspects of hydroponics according to writers' experiences.

Apart from reading manuals, you may also obtain valuable information by seeing discussion forums linked to hydroponic gardening online.

As soon as you have sufficient info and more importantly know your requirements or needs, then you may begin constructing your own hydroponic gardening strategy and also have fun using it.

Most Frequently Asked Hydroponic Gardening Questions

Before you can proceed and construct a hydroponic garden, you have to first understand just what it is and also the responsibilities and degree of commitment it involves. Hydroponics, essentially, describes the capability to grow plants from the lack of soil. Regardless of what science publications have taught us over time, all vegetables and plants do not need sunlight, air, and water to be able to flourish.

Below are just four of the most often asked questions by growers new to the notion of gardening:

"Can plants actually be grown indoors?"

Unlike what we have grown to understand about sun and its crucial role in assisting our crops grow, growing plants indoors through hydroponics is really possible.

To be able to grow plants inside you have to be conscious of how many additional supplies and growing techniques need to be put to use so as to grow plants correctly. As an instance, in hydroponics, your crops must maintain a particular temperature of 60 to 80 degrees Fahrenheit so as to grow to their fullest capacity. Furthermore, keeping your lawn's nutrient solution every day and having the capability to offer sufficient supplies of water is essential to keep your garden from withering away.

"How long will it take for my hydroponic garden to grow?"

Taking the first steps to beginning a hydroponic garden will require dedication, commitment, and above all, time. Unlike conventional gardens where you might observe seeds branching out in a few days, hydroponic gardens take more time to see expansion because the nutrient options and indoor lighting variables you have to work with are somewhat more complicated.

Furthermore, other variables you ought to take into account would be the kinds of hydroponic garden crops you would like to grow and how large you want your garden to be.

"How can my hydroponic plants get light"

Since you aren't growing plants out in copious quantities of sun, you will have to provide your hydroponic garden crops using artificial lighting by means of hydroponic grow light or lights bulbs. The degree of the lighting you supply your plants can also be crucial as you need to give enough heat from the bulbs to assist in your plants development - although not too much to greatly increase the warmth of your garden crops.

"Why should I start a hydroponic garden on a traditional garden?"

There are lots of benefits of beginning a hydroponic garden on a traditional garden that include:

- Ease of manageability to control the environment where your crops (or veggies) are growing
- Doesn't need copious quantities of water to cultivate
- Assurance of all your plants (or veggies) growing correctly
- Hardly any desire to participate in hard labor to till your garden
- Not necessary to buy pricey soil/fertilizer

In short, beginning a hydroponic garden is the perfect option if you're worried about providing the healthiest, most pesticide and contaminant-free air.

Pests and Diseases Control

Though hydroponic gardeners dodge a high number of plant issues from eschewing soil (which can be a home to some variety of plant creatures), pests and diseases still can wreak havoc from time to time. Botrytis, Cladosporium, Fusarium, and Verticillium ensure the majority of the genera of bacteria which may threaten your crops. The pests which could prove bothersome include aphids, caterpillars, cutworms, fungus gnats, leaf miners, nematodes, spider mites, thrips, and white flies.

A few good approaches to prevent infestation and disease are to:

- Always keep a sanitary growing environment
- Grow naturally chosen disease- and - pest-resistant plant types
- Maintain your growing region properly ventilated and in the right temperatures to your plants
- Keep a close eye on your plants accordingly if a problem does happen, you are able to act quickly

With insects, occasionally you're able to pull off and crush any big ones. Or you may attempt to scrub the infected crops with a mild soap solution (like Safer Soap).

If an issue gets out of control, it could be required to employ biological control in the way of a spray. Research which product will work best on your circumstances. Always follow the directions on pesticides really carefully. Alternately, there are quite a few management products available on the market nowadays that contain a botanical chemical or a component that's been synthesized from a plant substance.

On botanical substances as controlling agents:

Over the past few years, scientists from all over the globe have begun to have a closer look in any given chemicals within the plant kingdom which may hold the reply to our pest and disease management issues. A number of businesses have even changed from growing artificial pesticides into imitating character by synthesizing naturally occurring chemicals in a lab setting. Extracts of willow, cinnamon, grapefruit, garlic, neem, bittersweet, lemon grass, derris, eucalyptus, and tomato are useful in controlling pests and diseases.

pH

The pH of a nutritional supplement solution is a measurement of its relative concentration of hydrogen ions.

Negative hydroxyl ions are made by the manner systems filter and combine air into the nutrient alternative feeding crops. Plants nourish from an exchange of ions. As ions have been removed from the nutrient solution, pH increases. As a result, the more ions which are consumed from the plants, the larger the growth. A solution with a pH value of 7.0 comprises comparatively equivalent concentrations of hydrogen ions and hydroxyl ions.

After the pH is below 7.0, there are more hydrogen ions than hydroxyl ion. This type of remedy "acidic." After the pH is above 7.0, you will find fewer hydrogen ions than hydroxyl ions. This usually means that the remedy is "alkaline." Test the pH level of your nutritional supplement using a kit composed of vials and fluid reagents. These kits are available in local chemistry, hydroponic, nursery, garden provider, or even swimming pool supply shops.

It's also a fantastic idea to check the pH level of your water prior to adding any nourishment. If your answer is overly alkaline add some acid. Though such conditions rarely happen, there are times when you might need to decrease the degree of acidity. This may be done with the addition of potassium hydroxide (or potash) into the solution in tiny amounts until it's balanced once more.

Photosynthesis

Plants will need to absorb many necessary nutrients in the nutrient solution or in the case of conventional agriculture--the soil. However, plants may create a few of their food. Plants utilize the method of photosynthesis to make meals for energy. Carbohydrates are created from carbon dioxide (CO_2) and also a supply of hydrogen (H)--for example water--from chlorophyll-containing plant cells when they're exposed to light. This procedure leads to the creation of oxygen (O).

Plant Problems

Every now and again, you're certain to encounter an issue with your plants. This is but a reality of any kind of gardening. The trick is to act quickly, armed with caliber comprehension.

Mineral Deficiency

Symptoms Nitrogen Deficiency can cause yellowing of the leaves, particularly in the older leaves. The rise of new roots and shoots is stunted. In berries, the stalks may turn a purple color. A phosphorous deficiency is typically associated with dark green foliage and stunted growth.

As in nitrogen deficiency, the stalks may appear purple. But because the leaves are not yellowish as they are in nitrogen deficiency, the entire plant can turn a purplish green color. Iron deficiency leads to yellowing between the leaf veins. Compared to nitrogen deficiency, the yellowing start seems to come from the younger leaves. Following a prolonged lack of iron, then the leaves may turn completely white.

Wilting

This disease could be due to environmental factors or disorder (usually due to Fusarium). Nutrient and networking temperature could be adjusted to cure wilt. But if Fusarium has taken hold, the odds your plants will endure are low.

If wilting is due to ecological causes:

Attempt to spray the plants and roots with cool, clean water to rejuvenate them. If this has not helped them from the following day, try it. When the crops react, top-off the nutrient solution and also assess the pH. When the plants do not react to the misting, empty the tank, then move into a shadier place, then refill with trendy, refreshing nutrient solution. Do not reuse the old option --begin with fresh nutrients and water.

If wilting is because of some system congestion of nutritional supplement:

I've seen tomato plants which have been so dehydrated because of a nutrient source blockage they were lying flat and also for all of the world seemed stone-cold dead. After the nutrient stream resumed and the crops were saved from the stressful environment of night, they reappeared so nicely I wondered if I'd dreamed the prior day's "tragedy" The moral of the story is to always give plants an opportunity to rekindle, even if the situation appears impossible.

Propagation

Plants can be propagated by numerous methods. Growers can allow a plant go to seed, then collect the seeds, then start the cycle again (see germination). Another procedure is to take stem cells, which can be called cloning (since you're making a specific replica of the parent plant). Though this procedure will not work with all plants, it's an extremely effective technique.

Simply cut a side shoot at the very top of the primary shoot, only below an expansion node. Ensure there are two expansion nodes over the cut.

Eliminate any of the lower leaves close to the bottom of this new plant. This cutting edge can subsequently be suspended by putting it in water or in a growing medium (perlite works nicely) that's kept moist. The usage of a rooting hormone can aid your odds of succeeding.

Pruning

Remove any discolored, insect-eaten, or sick-looking leaves from plants. Pulling off several outer leaves or cutting off the top a plant can allow it to grow fuller. Use sharp scissors to prune your plants. At times you may wish to prune a plant to concentrate its energy on the rest of the shoots. Pruning is an art and should be carried out with caution. Damaged or dying follicles might also have to be pruned from time to time.

Soil

Never use soil during any facet of hydroponics. Should you ever go a plant by a soil-based scenario to hydroponics, eliminate all traces of soil or potting mix from the roots.

Soil holds tons of germs and other organisms and substances that need to grow in and hydrates your hydroponic system. A number of these can really parasitize your plants and impede its development.

This is another benefit of hydroponic growing: The plant could get on with growing without needing to support a multitude of different organisms as occurs in traditional soil growing.

Infection

Various plants have distinct germination and growing temperatures. Always ensure you assess each plant growing requirements--notably minimum and maximum humidity levels. Remember that certain types of plants might have different prerequisites.

Water

Since the water supply is the root of life for the crops, quality is crucial. All plants rely upon their ability to uptake water openly. Between 80 and 98% of the uptake is needed for transpiration (loosely compared to sweat in creatures), which permits the plant to create and marginally control its instantaneous microclimate. Plants also require clean, uncontaminated water to create their very own healthy food source.

The water you use in your hydroponic system has to be pure. It's almost always a great idea to check your water supply prior to incorporating nutrients so you are not adding a component that's already present.

In small systems, it would be sensible to use distilled water. If you're beginning a bigger hydroponic operation, it'd be a fantastic idea to have a water evaluation done. Factors like sodium chloride (salt, or NaCl) hardness and content will be of fantastic use to growers. Additionally, groundwater may have components usually not present in conditioned water. A vital bit of information: Get to know your water!

Avoiding Plant Diseases

Seeing healthful plants get ill and die is a really depressing sight to a gardener. Plant diseases are constantly on the market, waiting to attack your garden. While sonic diseases can easily be treated, other more serious diseases will require repeat treatments to take care of. Some diseases are so severe (tobacco mosaic virus for example), the plant is doomed. Plant diseases can severely lower crop production, even when the ill plants recover. Let's keep diseases from our gardens! Here is how:

Maintenance of Your Hydroponic Garden

The best defense against plant disease is to keep your plants healthy and actively growing, by making sure of good conditions in your garden.

Care to temperature, air movement and air change, good spacing of crops, constant growing conditions - these practices ensure healthful, stress-free plants which could withstand disease and pests nicely. Many times, disease and bugs will strike a feeble plant in your garden and grow armies to invade the rest of your plants that are healthy!

Sanitization:

Use Healthy Plant Stock
- A cutting out of a sick plant will take on the disorder from the new plant.
- Some forms of this plant will have higher natural immunity to disease in relation to their "weak sisters," when you can, grow just types that have proven disease resistance.

Keep Tools, Hands and Clothing Clean
- Diseases, pests and insect can travel to new host crops
- During pruning, transplanting and managing; wash your hands after handling diseased plants until you touch a healthful one
- Clean tools and knives nicely after use
- Keep garden clean of dead leaves

Sterilize Garden or other Grow Mediums

(a medium is exactly what your roots are growing in)

- This is particularly important if using garden soil in the garden in a container inside or if utilizing recycled rockwool or lava stone for fresh crops
- The soil-fewer potting mixes and fresh rockwool are believed to be clean currently - no additional therapy is required

Utilize R/O Water Distilled

- If you're worried about the prospect of disease on your own water, you will find a few easy procedures to deal with water and kill illness until you infect your garden:

Chlorine Bleach (1/4 Cup for 30 g)

- Add to water and stir well
- Add compost into water after treating it with bleach
- Utilize air pump and air stone to push off bleach and keep the water bubbly

Hydrogen Peroxide (35%) (1 tbsp. for 10 gallons)

- This item is water with additional oxygen, and also the energetic oxygen will kill illness in the water
- Add to water
- Stir well, then add compost

Note: Peroxide helps plants to consume food simpler and faster, so this therapy comes with an excess advantage to the garden.

Check your garden for issues and treat them immediately! You may remove the disease altogether, until it gains a foothold on your garden.

pH Acid base.

Chemical change effects from the creation of new materials; these substances could be useful or harmful (and sometimes both!). Two varieties of substances that are extremely essential in everyday life are acids and bases. Acids are sour, and water-soluble substances that are extremely helpful in industry, home cleaning agents, and cooking; a few instances are peppermint, vitamin C pills, club soda, aspirin, lemon juice and cream of tartar.

Vinegar is a solution of roughly one part lipoic acid to 20 parts water - such a combination of water and acid is known as an acidic solution. Lemons and grapefruit possess a flavor that is sour, since they feature an acid known as citric acid. Baking powder includes a sterile acid known as tartaric acid. One other essential acid is stomach acid (dilute hydrochloric acid) which assists in the digestion of our food.

Acids that are not diluted in warm water are harmful - they undergo chemical change so easily they can respond with skin and cause burns. Bases are sour, water-soluble substances that are also quite helpful. Examples of foundations are ammonia, baking soda, and drain cleaner. Bases can also be utilized in certain batteries. The solutions that they form with water are known as fundamental or alkaline solutions. Bases can also be highly reactive and have to be treated with extreme care, as they also respond readily with epidermis.

You've likely heard of antacids. These compounds are foundations that are safe to consume and with respond with stomach acid. A chemical change by which an acid reacts with a base is called neutralization. It's known as neutralization because equivalent quantities of acid and base generate a solution that is neutral - neutral acidic nor basic. Antacids are used when the gut contains an excessive amount of acid, which irritates the stomach lining.

The pH scale is a measure of how acidic or basic a solution is. This scale ranges from 0 to get a very acidic alternative to 14 to get a very basic solution. A neutral solution has pH 7. A reduction of one unit on this scale represents multiplying acidity ten times.

Most plants prefer a slightly acidic pH 6.0 - 6.5. Proper pH levels are essential for the plant to have the ability to consume all of the nutrient provided from the solution.

An overly high or very low pH is among the most typical issues associated with house hobby manufacturers. These issues show quickly and may be countered efficiently! Most town tap water has a slightly basic pH 7 - 8, so the nutritional supplement we combine to a solution is acidic established and will correct the pH a stage or so reduced. We might nevertheless need to correct down utilizing a secure, usable acid like a dilute phosphoric acid. This really is the most typical scenario.

Possibly the root of water we use is more contaminated (e.g. some well and ground waters) and after blending the nutrient we will need to correct the pH higher. In this case we'd use a secure, usable alkali like a dilute di-potassium phosphate. A very simple method may be employed to discover if a solution is acidic or basic. An index is a chemical that changes colour, depending upon whether it's put in an acidic solution or a fundamental solution.

Additionally, there are digital meters available to readily check pH levels in option. They are just dipped into the solution and provide an electronic read out.

Maybe among the most overlooked aspects of gardening, pH is quite essential in organic and pruning in addition to regular "soil" gardening. pH is measured on a scale of 1-14 with 7 being "neutral." Acids are lower than 7 and alkalis (bases) are over 7.

This section deals with the pH of hydroponic gardening and also the availability of nutrition at different pH levels in a soilless growing medium. Organic and grime gardening possess various degrees; hence the next graph does not pertain to them. To be technical, the term pH refers to the possible hydrogen-hydroxyl ion content of a remedy. Solutions ionize into negative and positive ions. In case the alternative has more hydrogen (positive) ions than hydroxyl (negative) ions subsequently it's an acid (1-6.9 about the pH scale). Conversely if the alternative has more hydroxyl ions than hydrogen it's alkaline (or base), with a variety of 7.1-14 on the pH scale.

Pure water contains an equilibrium of hydrogen (H+) and hydroxyl (OH-) ions and can be consequently pH neutral (pH 7). After the water is significantly less than it may have a pH either greater or lower than 7.

The pH scale is logarithmic, meaning that every unit of change equals a tenfold shift from the hydrogen/hydroxyl ion concentration.

To put it another way, a solution having a pH of 6.0 is 10 times more acidic than the usual alternative using a value of pH 7.0, and a solution with a pH value of 5.0 will be 10 times more acidic than the alternative of 6.0 pH and 100 times more acidic than a solution using a 7.0 pH. This implies that whenever you're adjusting the pH of your nutrient solution and you need to transfer it two points (illustration: 7.5 to 5.5) you may need to use 10 times longer adjuster than if you had been moving the pH Value only 1 point (7.5 to 6.5).

Why Is pH Important?

If the pH isn't at the suitable level than the plant will reduce its ability to absorb a few of those vital components necessary for healthy development. For many plants there's a specific pH degree which will produce optimal results (see graph 1 below). This pH level will differ from plant to plant, but generally most plants prefer slightly acid increasing surroundings (involving 6.0 - 6.5), even though most plants may still live in an environment having a pH of between 5.0 and 7.5. When pH increases above 6.5 a number of the nutrients and micro-nutrients start to precipitate from the solution and can follow the walls of the reservoir and growing chambers.

For instance: Iron will probably be approximately half an hour in the pH level of 7.3 and also at approximately 8.0 there's almost no iron left in the solution in any way. For your plants to utilize the nutrients they have to be dissolved in the solution. After the nutrition have precipitated from the solution your crops can't consume them and will endure (or perish). Some nutrition will precipitate from the solution once the pH drops also.

Checking pH

When you're growing hydroponically assessing and adjusting pH is a very simple matter, it could be somewhat more complex when expanding organically or in soil. There are lots of methods to look at the pH of the nutrient solution on your own system. Paper test strips are likely the most affordable method to check the pH of the nutrient solution. These newspaper strips are impregnated using a pH sensitive dye that changes color when dipped into the nutrient solution. The newspaper strip is then compared to a color chart to find out the pH level of the alternative being assessed. These test strips are cheap, but occasionally they are sometimes tough to read, since the colors differences may be subtle.

The pH Scale

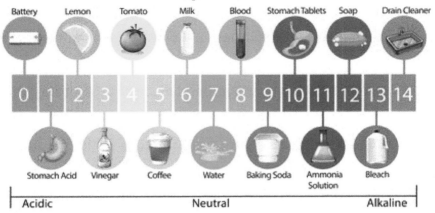

Liquid pH test kits have been possibly the most popular procedure to inspect pH for the hobby gardener. All these liquid test kits work with the addition of a couple drops of a pH sensitive dye into a little bit of the nutrient solution, then comparing the colour of the resulting liquid using a color graph. The liquid kits are somewhat more costly than the paper test strips but they also work really nicely, and are usually easier to "read" compared to paper index strips.

The most high-tech manner to assess pH is to utilize the electronic meters. These yards come in a massive selection of sizes and costs. The most popular kind of pH meter to the hobby gardener would be the electronic "pens." These pens are produced by a number of distinct companies and are extremely handy and user friendly. You only dip the electrode to the nutrient solution for a couple of moments and also the pH value is displayed on an LCD screen.

The pH meters are extremely accurate (when correctly calibrated) as well as quick. They will need to be cared for correctly or they will cease functioning. The glass bulb electrode has to be kept clean and moist constantly. The pH meters are in reality quite sensitive volt meters and therefore are vulnerable to difficulties using the electrode. The pH meters are somewhat temperature sensitive. A number of the pH yards available on the market have Automatic Temperature Compensation (ATC), which corrects the scanning connected to temperature. On yards without ATC the pH ought to be assessed at precisely the exact same time of day every time so as to minimize any temperature associated changes.

The pH meters generally have to be calibrated regularly, as the yards could "drift" and also to assure accuracy you need to assess calibration often. The tip has to be kept in an electrode storage option or in a buffer solution. The trick is that it shouldn't be permitted to dry out. On account of the fact that pH meters have a reputation of breaking down without warning it's a fantastic idea to maintain an emergency backup for assessing pH (paper test strips or a liquid pH test kit), just in case.

Adjusting pH

There are several chemicals utilized from the hobby gardener to correct pH. The most popular are likely phosphoric acid (to lower pH), and potassium hydroxide (to increase pH). Both these substances are relatively secure, even though they may cause burns and should never come in contact with the eyes. Most hydroponic supply shops sell pH adjusters which are diluted to a degree that's reasonably secure and user friendly.

Concentrated adjusters can cause big pH changes and may make adjusting the pH quite bothersome. A lot of different chemicals may be employed to correct the pH of hydroponic nutrient solutions. Nitric oxide and sulfuric acid may be used to reduce pH, but are a lot more harmful than phosphoric acid. Food grade citric acid is sometimes utilized in gardening to reduce pH.

Always add the nutrients into the water before assessing and adjusting the pH of your nutrient solution. The compost will normally reduce the pH of their water because of its chemical makeup. After incorporating nutrient and mixing the solution, check the pH with whatever way you've got. If the pH has to be corrected add the proper adjuster. Use small quantities of pH adjuster until you get knowledgeable about this procedure.

Recheck the pH and repeat the above steps until the pH level is where you desire it to be. The pH of the nutrient solution will have a propensity to go up since the plants use the nutrients.

Because of this the pH has to be assessed periodically (and corrected if needed). To begin I recommend that you assess pH on a daily basis. Each system will alter pH at a different speed based on various factors. The kind of growing medium used, the weather, type of crops and even the era of these plants all impact the pH variations.

Tips and Tricks for Growing Healthy Herbs and Vegetables

There's a whole selection of plants which may be grown using hydroponic gardening. Most crops could be increased using any of those hydroponic techniques. There are a number of that do better using a particular system. But they'll all do much better than when they had been growing by the standard soil approach. Now you have a better comprehension of the several hydroponic gardening methods, in addition to the nutrients and mediums to utilize, you'll have to select which crops you would like to grow. If you're just beginning, it's far better to begin with the smaller plants, like herbs. Large rooted plants may pose issues, like blockages, and the newcomer may not recognize it is occurring.

As a guideline, you can grow just about any vegetable or herb, employing the hydroponic system. Many fruits do nicely also, as do flowers. Often it may be a case of trial and error before you discover the very best system and harvest which fits your environment. As stated earlier in this publication, much depends upon your available space, budget, energy and time. People who grow in a greenhouse or outside might be more prone to pests. When growing in a room in your house, then it will not be such a problem because the crops are better shielded.

Other aspects, like nutrients, pH levels, humidity, temperature, light, and ventilation, all play their role in hydroponic growing. This next section will provide you an overall idea of the kinds of edible plants you can grow best in the many systems. Growing a huge array of blossoms, like tulips, may be achieved on a small scale for individual usage. Any seasonal species can be grown all year around.

Getting Started

If you're eager to grow edible plants, then proceed with those who are proven to perform well without having too much attention. Whenever you're restricted by distance and expertise, consider starting with the Wick System, where you are able to construct a smaller hydroponic garden. These hints are quickly growing, rather sturdy, and don't require a great deal of room.

Vegetable: Spinach, Bell Peppers, Lettuce, Tomatoes

Fruit: Strawberries

Herbaceous plants: Basil, Parsley

Beans are a hot weather vegetable which grows best in a hydroponic system. Seeds are planted in the expanding medium and watered from below from the grid. Seeds germinate in 16 days, and because green beans are very similar to other vegetable plants, no particular formula is necessary. They'll grow quickly, chubby, and flavorful!

Broccoli

Broccoli (in the plural of all broccolo, speaking to "the flowering top of a cabbage") is a plant of their mustard/cabbage family. Broccoli has big flower heads, generally green in colour, organized in a tree-like style on branches sprouting out of a thick, edible stem. The bulk of blossom heads is surrounded by foliage. Many kinds of broccoli are continuing. It's implanted in May to be chosen throughout winter or early the next year in temperate climates. It grows well in hydroponic systems but as it's a large plant, it demands sturdy staking.

Cabbage

Buy cabbage seedlings or grow your own from rockwool cubes.

When they grow big enough to stand by themselves, move them into the hydroponic pots and encircle the cubes using a growing medium. In case you've got a system, which utilizes "flushing"--fill out the tray from underneath with a flood of water, then drain it wait till your seedlings have grown big enough that they won't float from this medium. Cabbage may need up to two feet to grow, based on the variety.

Cauliflower

Cauliflower, a cruciferous vegetable, is at precisely the exact same plant family as broccoli, cabbage, kale, and collards. It's a streamlined head (known as a "curd"), with a mean size of six inches . It's made up of undeveloped blossom buds. The flowers are fixed to a central stalk. A sturdy service is crucial to keep all the roots from the hydroponic solution.

This may be achieved by using a coating of gravel by which the roots may get to the hydroponic nutrients, or putting up netting that enables the roots to grow. The hydroponic nutrients could be sent via drip irrigation twice each day. This is going to keep the roots from becoming too moist.

Broccoli and cauliflower are just two of the very cost-efficient vegetables to increase due to the lower temperatures needed and also the absence of need to always offer hydroponic nutrients.

Cucumber

Their speedy growth concerning the time accessible makes smoothies a fantastic candidate for a fall harvest. They are typically seeded in July, place in the greenhouse through the first week of August, also chosen in September to December. The cucumber responds just like a semitropical plant. It grows best under conditions of elevated humidity, humidity, and light intensity and also having an uninterrupted source of nutrients and water. Under positive and secure environmental and nutritional requirements and if pests are in check, the crops grow quickly and generate heavy amounts.

Eggplant

Eggplant must be planted in full sunlight. The plants can easily be hurt by frost and won't do well with extended periods of cool weather. Eggplants must be treated just like berries, the sole real difference being that eggplants enjoy it warmer. Plant them out of nursery stock, or begins, in the first spring. Allow 60-100 days to reach maturity.

Lettuce

Leaf lettuce or semi-headed lettuce would be the best kinds for hydroponic systems. Black-seeded Simpson, Boston, bibb or butter, or leaf lettuces are great options.

Lettuce demands extra light to grow successfully. It prefers cooler temperatures compared to warm weather plants. For optimum results, place your temperature controllers for 75 degrees Fahrenheit throughout the day and 55 degrees Fahrenheit during the night.

Peas

Snow peas like the warmer weather in the spring and autumn, but do not deal with the hot summertime well. The exact same is stated for lettuce, celery and many salad greens although they're somewhat more tolerant. Chinese peas, also referred to as snow peas are a cool season crop and therefore are sensitive to heat. Temperatures over 86 deg. F may cause poor growth. Before planting, you might wish to decide on the peas you wish to plant: English (garden), Chinese (snow) or Snap peas. English peas only produce seeds that are edible. Chinese peas create edible pods in addition to edible seeds, and snap beans do exactly the same. The beans will be ready to pick in about three weeks after the flowers begin to appear.

Peppers

Peppers, like berries, choose warm growing conditions.

Most carbohydrates plants also need staking. Suggested types to grow hydroponically consist of cubico, mazurka, Fellini, Nairobi and golden flame for sweet peppers and jalapeno, habanero and simmer for hot peppers. Light and temperature needs to grow peppers hydroponically are just like growing polyunsaturated fats.

Spinach

Start your seeds in rockwool. Put seeds into drilled holes and hang slightly over a hydroponic nutrient solution in an ebb and flow method. Germinating plants will need to be increased slightly to allow more oxygen to grow their roots, since the rockwool isn't a fantastic conductor inside this aspect. After the seeds have sprouted, transfer them into their permanent place. Permit twenty square inches for each plant. The hydroponic solution you are using at this stage are extremely critical since no growing medium is required with all the ebb and flow method. Plants are put on a netting-type substance with their roots allowed to dangle over the solution. Spinach won't flourish in an excessive amount of light.

Seasoned Grower

For the seasoned gardener, you might be daring and

contemplate growing plants that require more space and attention.

Explore growing with an Aeroponics system and begin plants which have bigger roots. It's much better to get a bigger system for plants that are more advanced. Root and tuber vegetables, like carrots, celery, and parsnips will require a great deal more attention and distance. For all those that have a bigger hydroponic garden, you can progress to the harder plants, like zucchini, or perhaps vining plants, however they do require distance. If you are more experienced, you can think about growing sunflowers, tobacco, shrubs, nut trees, as well as the prickly blackberry shrub.

How to Pick Hydroponics Plants to Grow from the Suburban Hydroponic Garden

The appealing part of hydroponics gardening, and also the main reason why so many commercial and home gardeners and farmers have been attracted to it is the rate the crops grow and the quantity of produce crops grown with hydroponics technologies.

Though it looks like it's a significant step from growing crops in land, the measure is really only rather small. The nutrients which would usually be included within soil are supplied in the water.

After this was completed, besides bodily support for your plant roots, the land provides no additional benefit. Since they receive each the components they get in soil, an enormous assortment of plants could be grown hydroponically.

The main kinds of hydroponics plants which we see are the ones we consume. You might have noticed that lots of types of herbs and lettuce are sold in supermarkets from legumes with their roots still attached. These plants are grown hydroponically. They are equally wholesome and delicious as plants grown in soil.

Strawberries

Hydroponic strawberries are a seasonal fruit, bearing fruit just through the warmer months of this year. Hydroponics technology, with the supply of nutrients, light, and water, can grow strawberries throughout the year, making abundant, reddish, luscious, sweet fruit. The expense of hydroponic gardening isn't any more costly than farming with soil, meaning that hydroponics strawberries could be offered to local supermarkets and markets all year round from a local grower, instead of getting them shipped in throughout the out-of-season weeks. This considerably lowers the price of those hydroponic plants.

A hydroponic system could be tailored to match any growing program; berries are ideal for hydroponic cultivation. Perfect nutrient and water levels are readily kept to generate plump, succulent, unblemished fruit.

Consistently use runners that are certified virus free. Gently remove the runners or fresh strawberry plant out of its container. Eliminate as much of the dirt as possible by gently massaging and firming the roots. Submerge the whole root system into a bucket of cold water for approximately ten minutes, then rinse branches under cold running water to remove any residual soil. Be careful to inflict as little harm as possible to the roots and tiny root hairs as a lot of breakage will seriously pressure crops and impair development.

Dry or fragile leaves and roots should be removed at the moment. Add enough of this growing medium to fill out the pot ensuring the crown of the strawberry is well over the surface. The crown demands light and refreshing air since it is where fresh leaves and blossoms grow. When underwater, the crown will probably mold causing the whole plant to perish. Add the bud into your hydroponic garden. After plants have finished fruiting and generated runners, then clip the runners in the mother plant and root utilizing standard rooting methods.

Once cuttings or runners have created a great root system, they need to endure a frightening procedure. This could possibly be achieved by placing rooted cuttings in a garage or chilly basement where temperatures stay between zero and 5C. Chilling can last anywhere from 10 days to five weeks depending upon when your next harvest is desired.

Additional berries could be grown hydroponically, but they occupy a terrific deal of space, and you may need to dedicate yourself to handling your own garden for berry growing. It could be achieved, but it isn't among the simpler things.

The five best plants to grow within a hydroponic system are:

1. Lettuce

2. Spinach

3. Strawberries

4. Bell Peppers

5. Herbs

Cultivators have discovered these plants adhere to hydroponics just like a duck to water. They are powerful, fast growing and do not take a large quantity of effort to start -- every incredible part that provides another manufacturer a bit of wiggle room!

Now let's look at all these:

Lettuce in Hydroponics

Lettuce (and most other lush greens) should work as the first plant to launch with a hydroponic construction. These crops have a shallow root structure which matches with their brief over the ground elevation. That infers there is no persuasive motivation to tie stakes or putting in helpers for the plant. Or perhaps, you just have them grow while changing their improvement match program. In the long-term, they'll seem satisfactory to consume, and also you can!

- Grow time: About 30 times
- Greatest pH: 6.0 to 7.0
- Hint: Stagger plantings so you've got an unending load of early afternoon lettuce!
- Variety options: Romaine, Boston, Iceberg, Buttercrunch, and Bibb

Spinach in Hydroponics

Spinach grows fast in a hydroponic method, especially when utilizing the Nutrient Film Technique or different procedures that maintain the enhancement plan is considerably oxygenated. You will moreover use much less water compared to an in-the-ground garden. It is definitely not difficult to begin these plants from seed and oftentimes in the aftermath of growing, move them in your system.

- Grow time: About 40 days
- Greatest pH: 6.0 to 7.5
- Hint: For better spinach, maintain your temperatures between 65 degrees F and 72 degrees F. The reduced temperatures can slow growing time, be that as it may.
- Variety choices: Savoy, Bloomsdale, Smooth Leafed, Regiment, Catalina, Tyee, and Red Cardinal

Strawberries in Hydroponics

The most exceptionally thing about berries is how incidental they are. If you do not get them locally whenever the return is readied, you are relying upon trucked-in berries which begin self-destructing when they are picked. With hydroponics, you might have a ready to-eat collection of strawberries throughout the entire year. Gathering is super-useful too -- no twisting around! Strawberries appear to perform better with a to and for growth construction, and substantial water cultivation or supplemental support can go far to produce benefits.

• Grow time: Around 60 days
• Greatest pH: 5.5 to 6.2
• Hint: Do not purchase strawberry seeds, which will not be ready for a long time period. Or perhaps, you need to purchase cold-set off sprinters which are currently ready.
• Variety alternatives: Brighton, Chandler, Douglass, Red Gauntlet, and Tioga

Ring Peppers in Hydroponics

Ring peppers are an additional vine plant. Do whatever it takes to not let them reach their full stature, instead prune and subdue crops at about 8 slips to spike pepper development.

Substantial water culture or to and for growth methods would be best for peppers.

- Grow time: Around 90 days
- Greatest pH: 6.0 to 6.5
- Hint: Plan to provide around 18 hours of light for all these plants every day, and boost your lighting stand as the plants produce, maintaining plants about 6 wet layers in the lights.
- Variety choices: Ace, California Wonder, Vidi, and Yolo Wonder

Herbs in Hydroponics

There is a broad group of herbs which work brilliantly in hydroponic planting. Various studies have revealed that hydroponic herbs are more amazing and sweet-smelling than those born within the specialty. What herb would you wish to produce? Basil, chives, cilantro, dill, mint, oregano, parsley, rosemary, thyme, and watercress are by and large astonishing different choices. Herb creation is just another conceivable method to test out your new hydroponic system, and roughly with each construction design is reasonable to produce a development of herbaceous plants as you become familiar with the principles!

- Grow time: Varies by plant

• Greatest pH: Varies by plant

• Hint: Flush your growing medium about once weekly to shed some additional improvements your plants have not (or will not) acclimatize.

• Variety choices: Name your best selection, and you're going to discover guidelines for making it!

Different Yields are:

1. Lettuces

Favorable Temp: Trendy. pH: 6.0 - 7.0

Lettuces, the ideal component for your serving of mixed greens for your own kitchen, are probably the most widely perceived vegetables that are grown in Hydroponics. They grow exorbitantly lively in a hydroponic system and therefore are really simple to control. Lettuces can be produced in almost any Hydroponics system, such as the NFT, Aeroponics, Ebb and Flow, etc.

2. Tomatoes

Favorable Temp: Hot. pH: 5.5 - 6.5

Different sorts of berries, including cherry and other kinds, have been grown for the most part by Hydroponic experts and business cultivators. Ordinarily, the tomato is a natural thing, anyhow most importantly whether sellers or buyers believe it is a vegetable. One thing to remember is that berries demand a lot of light. So be put up to find some produce lights in case you need to grow them indoors.

3. Radishes

Favorable Temp: Trendy. pH: 6.0 - 7.0

Radishes are just another vegetable which makes an OK upgrading blend with numerous vegetables. Radishes are probably the least demanding vegetable to grow - both in soil and hydroponics. It is more intelligent to begin from seeds, also you'll be able to observe seedlings within 3 - 7 days. Radishes thrive in cool temperatures and also you should not waste time with any lighting.

4. Kale

Perfect Temp: Cool to hot. pH: 5.5 - 6.5

Kale is a particularly nutritious and wonderful ready plant for house and bistro dishes. It's a staggering vegetable to get a strong person with demonstrated curative favorable conditions. The excellent news is that individuals have grown Kale hydroponically for countless decades, so you can certainly do it with the water system. Moreover, frankly, it is definitely not difficult to grow and flourishes well within this structure.

5. Cucumbers

Favorable Temp: Hot. pH: 5.5 - 6.0

Cucumbers are a trivial vining plant that's produced in the home and at the company nurseries. They welcome a fast progress under adequate state and from that time forward give unbelievably noteworthy returns. There are two or three kinds and sizes of cabbage, for instance, extreme American slicers, long readily influenced seedless European, and also the smooth-cleaned Lebanese cocktails. All can grow nicely in Hydroponics. Cucumber is a hot plant so be certain that you provide it with sufficient temperature and light.

6. Spinaches

Outstanding temp: cool to heat. pH: 6.0 - 7.0

The most loved vegetable which will be eaten raw or arranged on your dinner plate grows nicely in a water-based condition. Spinach is a plant that is cool, therefore it does not need an on the top kind of lighting. You can collect it concurrently or pick a few leaves. You may get up to 12 months of decided collecting below a not too awful state of growing and climate condition.

7. Beans

Favorable Temp: Hot. pH: 6.0

One of the very advantageous and low-bolster veggies which may be grown hydroponically. You can select the kinds of beans you may produce, such as green beans, pinto beans, or lima beans. You will need a trellis or something to assist the plants in the event you plant legumes. Seed germination normally requires 3 - 8 days. Harvesting begins after 6 - 8 weeks. Beginning now and in the near future, you may keep on with the benefit for three to four months.

Herbs

8. Chives

Favorable temp: Hot. pH: 6.0

It is simpler to grow chives out of a plant in a hydroponic construction. It is so much better to get them from what the regional nursery provides. Below a standard growing condition, it requires six to about 8weeks until it's wholly grown. By then it's possible to secure it normally - it requires 3 - after a month to completely regrow. Chives need tons of lighting, 12 - 14 hours of light daily.

9. Basil

Favorable Temp: Hot. pH: 5.5 - 6.5

Basil thrives very nicely in a hydroponic method, also it's possible to create certain kinds of the very established herbs in Hydroponics. You can grow basil in NFT or a Drip construction. At the stage when this plant lands in the produce bin, you collect and cut it step by step. Basil needs tons of lighting. It'll encounter a bad growth level whenever you don't outfit it with over 11 hours of lightning.

10. Mints

Favorable Temp: Hot. pH: 5.5 - 6.5

Mints, for the large part peppermint and spearmint, have been grown widely both in soils and hydroponics. Their fragrant combinations in mints are resuscitating sharp, which reveals their use for a flavoring for sustenance and drinks. Mint roots propagate so fast, which makes it perfect to produce in Hydroponics.

Herbs

Many herbaceous plants will grow well in a hydroponic setting. Some that do the very best include anise, basil, catnip, chamomile, chervil, chives, cilantro, coriander, dill, fennel, lavender, marjoram, mint, lavender, parsley, lavender, lavender, thyme and tarragon.

Anise

Anise is a feathery annual that grows between 1 to 2 feet high, has cut serrated leaves and quite small, whitish flowers in flat clusters. Both the seeds and leaves have a hot, sweet ginger flavor. It grows quickly from seed and needs to be planted after all danger of frost has passed. The green leaves may be trimmed whenever plants are big enough and seeds might be accumulated one month following flowers blooming. Anise leaves may be used in salads and as a garnish; the seeds flavor confections like cakes and biscuits.

Basil

In a secure environment, growing basil can be achieved through the year. After maturing, it can be picked and trimmed each week. It reacts exceptionally well to hydroponic growing.

Cannabis

A psychoactive herb rotated from the flowering tops of berry plants. Cannabis is regulated under Schedule I of the Controlled Substances Act of 1970. It's likewise referred to as bhang, ganja, grass, hashish, marijuana, pot, reefer, tea, and marijuana. It thrives and grows to a vigorous plant in a hydroponic system. Many cannabis plants cultivated from America start to flower by late August to early October and the plants are harvested from October to November.

Catnip

It grows well in hydroponics in sunlight or partial shade. It's a perennial herb of the mint family which may grow from 3-5 feet tall. It's readily propagated by seed, stem cuttings, or rootball branch. Seed ought to be sown late in autumn or early in the spring. Sow in plugs or seeds 12 to 15 months prior to purchase. Seeds to completed plugs, 8 to 10 weeks; plugs to saleable crops, 3 to 5 months.

Chamomile

It growing nicely in soilless culture. It's used to make chamomile tea also owns lots of medicinal properties. Chamomile increased outdoors prefers full sun but will tolerate some shade. From seeds to completed plugs, 6 months; plugs to saleable crops 4 to 6 months.

Chervil

Chervil is a very low light cool temperature harvest. At temperatures over 70-75F, the plant will increase gradually and bolt to blossom from a young age. Cool roots are crucial to ensure decent growth. Unless shade and distinctive cooling system is utilized, chervil isn't easy to grow in the summertime. Growing time to crop is 4 months. It's the best winter harvest. Best grown under low lights.

Chives

Chives (a relative of the onion family) need a small space and create a constant source of seasoning for salads, and main dishes. Plants are hardy, endure a number of growing conditions, are extremely aromatic and coveted by gourmet cooks.

Cilantro

Cilantro (a relative of parsley) is a really successful tasting herb. It tolerates various pH requirements and reduced light conditions. It requires very little maintenance and reaches crop phase within fourteen days. It has to be regularly trimmed or it'll go to seed.

Coriander

Cilantro is a parsley-type herb. When grown for just leaves, it's known as cilantro but when permitted to keep on growing to seed, then it becomes what's referred to as coriander. Coriander needs cool temperatures or it will bolt. Coriander grows best in full sun. Just the immature leaves are all offered. (The older "feathery" leaves which precede bolting aren't desired.) To increase into a slab: upon final harvest, then pull plants out from the roots and re-seed or transplant. Harvest by cutting shirts to crown and enabling them to re-grow or pull up from the roots.

Dill

Dill is a tasty improvement for hydroponic herb gardens and it generates new growth when picked.

Replacing spent plants using fresh seedlings every few weeks will guarantee a continuous supply of dill. The streamlined fern foliage variety produces an abundance of lush expansion hence permitting for many cuttings from one plant.

Fennel

Fennel is a perennial (but generally grown as an annual) that grows to approximately 3 to 4 ft. tall. The leaves are divided into thread-like sections and resemble Dill and are light green. It grows quickly from seeds planted in spring and grows better in full sun. Plants have to be staked when 18 inches tall. Harvest seeds when mature. Pick the flower stalks before they blossom so they are ideal for eating. Fennel seeds are used as a condiment. The leaves have an anise-like taste and the stalks can be eaten like celery. Seeds may be utilized in cheese spreads and vegetable dishes.

Flowers

Growing flowers lends itself superbly to hydroponic gardening because they are sometimes grown in larger amounts, and may be grown year-round. Most flowers will succeed in a hydroponic garden, also if seedlings are large enough, flowers may be cut or transplanted.

Lavender

Frequent name for a genus of fragrant shrubs or herbs that's grown as a decorative plant in the garden and also for its sweet odor when dried. The dried flowers are utilized to fill sachets and also to perfume linens or clothing. Commercially they, along with the green components, are utilized for growing "oil of spike," aromatic vinegar, along with lavender oil. True lavender isn't fully hardy in northern gardens. It's located more in the milder Pacific Coast and in the South. As seed generates unstable plants, propagation is usually by cuttings of plants that are selected. Sow seeds 20 to 26 weeks prior to purchase; seeds to completed plugs, 12 to 16 weeks; plugs to saleable plant, 8 to 10 weeks.

Marjoram

 A perennial herb generally grown as an annual for its aromatic foliage used to flavor meat and shellfish dishes. It thrives in full sun. Considering that the seed is quite small, it's best sown in flats in the greenhouse and the seedlings transplanted out after all risk of frost has passed. Seeds to completed plugs, 6 months; plugs to saleable plant, two to four weeks.

Mint

Even though they are normally grown on property, many mints are in reality aquatic or semi-aquatic plants, doing their best in shallow water in the edges of rivers and streams. Among its adaptations to water would be to spread by stolons that go out across the surface of the ground or just beneath the surface. Spearmint, peppermint, and orange mint are 3 kinds of mints that grow best in or near water. Mint grown in water will have larger, more verdant foliage compared to land-grown mint, therefore it's perfect in hydroponic gardens.

Oregano (Wild marjoram)

Oregano is a hardy perennial which has sprawling stems which can grow to two feet tall. It has small white or pink blossoms.

Oregano may be propagated by division or seed. Stimulate foliage by cutting flowers. Replant when plants become woody in 3-4 years. Leaves can be preserved by drying or used fresh. Oregano leaves are utilized widely as a flavoring on pizza, or sprinkled over lamb. Used liberally in Italian-type sauces.

Parsley

Parsley, is an herb well suited to hydroponic growing.
As it has a very long tap root, the hydroponic container needs to be at least 12 inches deep to get the very best outcomes.

Rosemary

A hardy evergreen sub-shrub grown largely for its aromatic leaves which are employed in seasoning and produce an oil formerly utilized in medicine. Little light blue blossoms are borne in April or May. The leaves are white and woolly on both sides and dark and polished over. Plants might grow to a height of 6 ft and continue for a long time but need protection against the cold. It prefers alkaline soil and full sunlight, but does tolerate medium color. Sow in seed flats 22 weeks prior to purchase in 10 cm diameter pots. Seeds to completed plugs, 12 weeks; plugs to saleable crops, 10 weeks.

Sage

Frequent name for a rugged sub-shrub that's widely grown for seasoning dressings utilized with rich meats, as well as for flavoring sausages and cheese. In hydroponics, it may be grown from seeds protected from cold and it prefers sunlight. As the plants frequently exceed 3 ft in diameter, so they ought to be increased at least that way apart.

Sage leaves must be picked before flowering and dried out in a living area on displays or in a commercial drier, away from direct sunshine and then keep in airtight containers. Sow in seed or tin apartments 12 to 14 months prior to purchase. Seeds to completed plugs, 8 months; plugs to saleable crops 4 to 6 months.

Tarragon

A perennial herb that the leaves of which can be used for seasoning, particularly peppermint. Tarragon grows to three or two feet tall and enjoys medium sunlight, preferring some shade during the hottest portion of the day. Tarragon, during growth, appears to have little odor; nonetheless after the tops or leaves are picked, the oils focus and get started emitting their distinctive tarragon sweet odor. Plugs to saleable crops, 7 days.

Thyme

A plant in the mint family long cultivated and appreciated as a sweet herb. It's little lavender or pink blossoms and is increased as a border plant, such as decoration, or as an herb for use for seasoning. Thyme must be planted in early spring. It's quite sturdy and will grow under most states. It prefers full sunlight. Thyme needs minimal fertilization when grown in a hydroponic system. Sow in plugs 12 to 14 months prior to purchase. Seeds to completed plugs, 6 to 8 weeks; plugs to saleable crops 4 to 6 months.

Watercress

Low growing and monitoring European perennial. It's easily grown from seed. Its normal season is mid-autumn until spring. Following its flower buds appearance the leaves become overly position in taste to be edible. It's also easily grown inside in a hydroponic system. Start plants by sowing gently in containers filled with a medium. Watercress has many culinary, cosmetic, and medicinal applications.

Conclusion

Now that you've studied a number of the fundamental needs of every system, I expect you are feeling you have enough information to select the perfect hydroponic system and the appropriate plants for you. There'll be barriers along the way; some other kind of growing isn't without a set of issues. If you're aware of the pitfalls, then you will be prepared to counter them if they occur. Whether you choose to get started using a large or a tiny hydroponic system, there's absolutely not any requirement to break your back digging up soil.

My first tip to you is to begin with small rooted and fast-growing plants, like lettuce or herbs. That way, you'll be fast to reap the advantages of your labor of love. That first harvest will spur you on to larger and better things. The benefit of hydroponics is you will yield a harvest fast, provided you do it correctly. There's a wide selection of plants that could be grown with hydroponic technology. The most common hydroponic plants which we as consumers encounter are lettuce, berries, herbs, and naturally, tomatoes.

Hydroponics supplies these plants with the equilibrium in expansion conditions they need in order to grow quickly and get the most produce, which makes the whole system economically viable. I expect you're spurred on by my own excitement and feel encouraged to begin.

Lightning Source UK Ltd.
Milton Keynes UK
UKHW020630190421
382237UK00001B/135